511 Easy Wild Game RECIPES

511 Easy Wild Game RECIPES

Chef Gahagan

ISBN: Softcover 978-1-4535-6732-6

This book was printed in the United States of America.

To order additional copies of this book, contact:
Chef Gahagan
1 516 629-6052
www.chefgahagan.com

CONTENTS

PREFACE

Important – Read this first: How to Prepare Wild Boar

Wild Game, when cooked like Supermarket meat can be a very tough and gummy tasting meat unless you tenderize it and clean the taste. The best way to do this is to marinate it in Buttermilk and Meat Tenderizer for about three hours.

Buttermilk and Yogurt contain an enzyme that cleans the taste and tenderizes the meat. Be particularly careful of Wild Boar and venison. Both can be very tough when overcooked but mouthwateringly delicious when properly handled and prepared.

TASTE ENHANCERS

This all started with my making suggestions to a young bride. I was trying to make her cooking struggles a little easier. These are all simple suggestions.

Taste Enhancers

There are six basic Taste Enhancers in cooking. These are: Salt, Sugar, Sour, Bitter, alcohol and Glutamate. The first four you taste in your Mouth. The fifth, Alcohol, you taste in your nose and the sixth, Glutamate, as in MSG you taste in your stomach.

Salt

Basically, you want to have the same salt level as your body. If you raise the salt level of a dish more than 20% higher than that of your body, your body will reject it as too salty. Lower the salt level of a dish more than 20% less than your body and it will be rejected as tasteless.

Also, it helps to know that salt and sugar counteract each other. If you put in too much salt, you can counteract the slip by adding sugar.

Sugar

Sugar is an enormous taste enhancer. You want to add enough sugar to enhance the taste but not so much as to make the food taste sweet.

Sour

Citric acid such as found in lemon and orange juice is probably the most well known Sour taste enhancer. It counteracts the oily taste of many foods, Avocado and Olive oil for example, by stimulating your taste buds and making your mouth water.

Bitter

Acetic acid such as found in Cider and Wine Vinegar is the most well known Bitter taste enhancer. It counteracts the oily taste of many foods, Olive oil in salads for example, by stimulating your taste buds and in low concentrations, making your mouth water. In these respects, its action is very similar to "sour" or citric acid.

Alcohol

Alcohol has no flavor of its own and acts as an enormous taste enhancer in two very different ways.

1. It lowers your blood sugar levels and make you hungry.
2. Because of its high volatility alcohol intensifies and rapidly wafts flavors from your mouth to you nasal passages where they can be smelled.

MSG (Mono Sodium Glutamate)

MSG is NOT an artificial chemical. It is a naturally occurring sodium salt discovered by the Japanese in seaweed in the early 1900s. It is also an important neurotransmitter. MSG acts in the stomach sending signals to the brain that say "This food is delicious". Your mouth begins to water and the taste buds become more sensitive. Ripe tomatoes, Parmesan Cheese and Meat Stocks all owe much of their flavor appeal to naturally occurring MSG.

Two Examples:

This is why you see these six enhancers on the ingredient lists for so many prepared foods. It also explains the great appeal of a wine sauce. acid alcohol sugar (in some form) and MSG (Accent) in almost every prepared food on a Supermarket shelf.

An Example #1: Enhancing a Squash

Cook an acorn squash, take out the seeds and add a tbsp. of cordial (or rum with a 1/4 tsp. sugar) to the center. You will be amazed by how the alcohol and sugar enhance the taste.

Example #2: Make a quick Easy Wine Sauce

Keep a bottle of inexpensive Port or sweet Sherry wine by you stove. When you pan fry hamburger, lamb chops, steak, etc., deglaze (scrape up) the pan with port wine and pour it over the meat. Add a quarter tsp. Of MSG and you have a great wine sauce.

This gives you a great meat/wine sauce.

CHEF'S SUGGESTIONS

Question: How can I tell when the taste is right?
Answer: The only way you can tell when the Taste Enhancers are right is to taste the dish yourself. That is why you see so many pictures of chefs bending over pots, tasting, tasting, tasting.

Question: How can I remove the gamey flavor fro wild game?
Answer: Marinate it overnight in buttermilk or yogurt and meat tenderizer. Buttermilk and yogurt both have enzymes that remove the gamey flavor. They also tenderize meat. Stab a fork into the meat to encourage absorption. Be sure to thoroughly wash off the residue and do not ad salt. The commercial meat tenderizers are already full of salt.

Question: How can I tell how tough the meat is?
Answer: This is easy, bite it.

Question: How Can I Best Tenderize Tough Meat?
Answer: Marinate it overnight in buttermilk or yogurt and meat tenderizer. Buttermilk and yogurt both have enzymes that tenderize meat. They also clean the taste. Stab a fork into the meat to encourage absorption. Be sure to thoroughly wash off the residue and do not ad salt. The commercial meat tenderizers are already full of salt.

Question: Too much Salt or Sugar?
Answer: Salt and sugar will balance each other to some extent. So, if you put in too much salt, add sugar. If you put in too much sugar, add salt. And you can always add water, milk or stock to dilute the sauce.

But first WAIT, because salt and sugar are most intense when you first add them (They are only in the sauce). Wait a bit and they will be absorbed into the meat, beans or vegetables and the salty/sweet taste will disappear. The same holds true for Accent.

Question: Too much Accent?
Answer: Again wait. Then try adding more sugar. If that does not work, dilute the sauce. DON'T add more salt.

Question: How important are: Sea Salt, Kosher Salt, Raw Sugar, Fresh Ground Pepper, etc.
Answer: Forget them. Salt is salt. Sugar is sugar. Pepper is pepper, etc.

A Few Tips about Flavors

Herbs

Seasonings loose their flavor as they age so use good quality seasonings. Herbs also release their flavors slowly when cooking so do not expect an immediate result.

Minced Garlic

Don't bother mincing garlic. Use garlic powder instead.

Parsley Flakes

Use parsley flakes only as a decoration. Forget it for flavor. All the flavor in parsley is in the stems, not the leaves.

Gravy

If you make a pot roast, a osso bucco or a lambshank and you put in vegetables for flavor, take out the meat, pour off the fat and then blend the stock with the vegetables on high. This makes a delicious, gravy that uses the vegetables as a natural thickener instead of flour. P.S. It is also easier.

Make it Easy on Yourself

There are great commercial prepackaged sauces available. For example, use red clam sauce to cook fish. Use spaghetti sauce instead of plain tomato sauce to flavor meat loaf. Use packaged white (Bernaise) sauce instead of making your own. Use shrimp soup with a couple of cooked shrimp thrown in to create a fish dish.

Here are some easy delicious sauces for Wild Game (or any meat).

Cumberland Sauce

Cumberland Sauce was invented by the English Royal Duke of Cumberland for his Grouse and Venison. It is the most Elegant Meat Sauce in the world.

Ingredients

1 tsp. Dry Mustard
1 tbsp. Brown Sugar
1/2 cup Blackberry Jam
1/2 tsp. Ginger
1/4 tsp. Cloves
1 1/2 cup Port Wine
1/2 cup raisins
2 tsp. Cornstarch
2 tbsp. Water
1 tbsp. Grated orange rind

Directions

Mix Cornstarch and water; simmer till thickened and mix all ingredients together

Apricot Sauce

Ingredients

4-5 Fresh Apricots
1/2 tsp. Ginger
1/2 tsp. Cinnamon
2 tbsp. Sugar or to taste
1/2 tsp. MSG

Remove pits. Blend everything on high

Peach Sauce

Ingredients

2-3 Fresh Peaches
1/2 tsp. Ginger
1/2 tsp. Cinnamon
2 tbsp. Sugar or to taste
1/2 tsp. MSG

Directions

Remove pits. Blend everything on high.

Nectarine Cream Sauce

Ingredients

2-3 Fresh Nectarines
1/2 tsp. Ginger
1/2 tsp. Cinnamon
1/2 cup Heavy Cream
2 tbsp. Sugar or to taste
1/2 tsp. MSG

Directions

Remove pits. Blend everything on high.

Peaches and Cream Sauce

Ingredients

2-3 Fresh Peaches
1/2 tsp. Ginger
1/2 tsp. Cinnamon
1/2 cup Heavy Cream
2 tbsp. Sugar or to taste
1/2 tsp. MSG

Directions

Remove pits. Blend everything on high.
Heat to thicken

Wine Sauce #1

2 tbsp. Meat Stock or Pan residue
1 cups Port Wine
1/4 tsp. Garlic Powder
1/4 tsp. Tarragon
1/4 tsp. Thyme

Directions

Use one half the wine to deglaze the pan.
Mix all ingredients. Let stand until herbs soften

Blackberry Wine Sauce

2 tbsp. Meat Stock or Pan residue
1 cups Port Wine
1 cup Blackberry Jam
1/4 tsp. Garlic Powder
1/4 tsp. Tarragon
1/4 tsp. Thyme

Florentinene (spinach) Sauce

1 package frozen Cream Spinach

Sicilian Sauce

2 tbsp. Meat Stock
2 cups your favorites Pasta Sauce
1 tsp. Garlic Powder
2 tsp. Oregano
1/2 tsp. MSG
2 tbsp. Tomato Paste

Creamy Orange Sauce

1 can Frozen Orange Juice
1 cup Heavy Cream

Orange Sauce

1 jar Orange Marmalade
1 tbsp. Orange Zest (Grated Orange rind)
2 tsp. Cornstarch
1/2 cup Water

Directions

Mix Cornstarch and Water and heat until thickened. Mix all ingredients together. Let stand 1/2 hour. Strain before using.

Meat Stock Sauce

1 Pint Meat Stock
1 Cup Port Wine
2 tsp. Garlic
2 tsp. Thyme
1 tsp. Tarragon
1 tsp. Sugar
1 tsp. MSG
Pepper to taste
1 tsp. Thyme

Sauce Gahagan

1 Cup Mayonnaise
1 tbsp. Dijon Mustard
1 tsp. Soy Sauce

Sauce Gahagan #2

4 tbsp. Dijon Mustard
4 tbsp. Tomato Paste
2 tbsp. Catsup

Our Own White Sauce

3 tbsp. Flour
3 tbsp. Bacon Fat
1 cup milk
Salt and Pepper to taste

Directions

Mix flour and Bacon Fat into a roux.
Slowly add milk and then taste to adjust seasonings.

Our Own Basic Hunters' Sauce

3 tbsp. Flour
3 tbsp. Bacon Fat
1 cup meat stock
Salt and Pepper to taste

Directions

Mix flour and Bacon Fat into a roux
Mix flour and Bacon Fat into a roux over low heat. Slowly add Meat Stock and Port wine: taste to adjust Seasonings

Our Own Elegant Hunters' Sauce

4 tbsp. Flour
3 tbsp. Bacon Fat
1/2 cup meat stock
1/2 cup Port wine
Salt and Pepper to taste

Directions

Mix flour and Bacon Fat into a roux over low heat. Slowly add Meat Stock and Port wine: taste to adjust Seasonings

Sauce Alb.ert

Basic Hunter's sauce (as above). Blend in
1 tbsp. Tomato paste

Our Own Elegant Hunters' Sauce

4 tbsp. Flour
3 tbsp. Bacon Fat
2 cups meat stock
1 tbsp. Parmesan cheese
1/2 cup Port wine
Salt and Pepper to taste

Directions

Mix flour and Bacon Fat into a roux over low heat. Slowly add Meat Stock, Port wine and other ingredients. Taste to adjust Seasonings

Orange Sauce

1 container Frozen Orange Juice
1 Half Pint (1 cup) Heavy Cream
1 tsp. MSG

ALLIGATOR RECIPES

important—read this first:

Chef Gahagan says always marinate meat in Buttermilk and Meat Tenderizer for about three hours. Then wash off the buttermilk and remarinate in wine and herbs if desired.

Alligator

Ingredients

1 pound alligator meat
4 eggs,
1 cup flour
1/2 cup butter seasoned salt and pepper to taste

Directions

Wash off Buttermilk marinade.

Remove any fat and cut meat into bite size pieces. Cover the alligator pieces flour then dip the pieces into beaten eggs.

Gently sautethe pieces until golden brown on both sides. Serve with Dijon Mustard Sauce. Decorate with lemon wedges and parsley.

Dijon Mustard Sauce
1 cup mayonnaise
1 tablespoon Dijon mustard
1 teaspoon soy sauce
1 teaspoon lemon juice

Grilled Cajun Style Gator

Marinate meat in a mix of Buttermilk and tenderizer.
Ingredients
4 lbs. Gator Tail scissored into bite size pieces
1 cup butter
Cajun Seasoning Mix:
2 tbsp. Garlic powder
2 tbsp. Chili Powder
2 tsp. oregano Powder
1 tbsp. Cumin
1 tbsp. thyme
1 tbsp.each Salt and Pepper
4 tbsp. Paprika

Directions

Mix all seasonings together.

Roll each piece of gator in the mixture. Cook on high on a barbecue grill or broil for 4 to 6 minutes, or until gator meat is white and forks firm.

Serve warm with lemon wedges.

ANTELOPE

important—read this first:

Chef Gahagan says, always marinate meat in Buttermilk and Meat Tenderizer for about three hours. Then wash off the buttermilk and remarinate in wine and herbs if desired.

Barbecued Antelope Ribs

1 Quart Buttermilk
6 lb. Antelope ribs with some loin meat attached
Red Wine sufficient to cove ribs in a marinade 1 1/2 c Water
1 cup Currant or plum jelly or jam
1/2 Brown sugar
1/4 md Onions, finely diced
1/8 tsp.cloves
1/2 tsp.dry mustard 1/2 tsp. garlic powder 1/2 ts Salt
Black pepper and salt to taste

Directions

Marinate Ribs in buttermilk for two hours with 1 tsp. Meat tenderizer. Then wash off buttertmilk

Preheat oven to 325 degrees. Combine all ingredients except the ribs in a large bowl. Blend well and sprinkle ribs with pepper and additional salt.

Place in 5 qt. roasting pan in double layer. Roast 1 hour.

Pour sauce over ribs. Increase heat to 350 degrees and bake until ribs just begin to char on top, about 1 1/2 hours. Turn ribs over cover pan and bake about 30 minutes longer, until ribs are tender and sauce is thick (If necessary, add water). To serve, place ribs on serving platter. Pour sauce over ribs. Makes about 6 servings.

Barbecued Antelope Chops

20 Antelope chops
6 oz Beer
1 large. Onion, chopped and sauteed
4 pats of butter
2 oz Garlic Salt

Directions

Place aluminum foil on hot grill with sides folded up, so there is no runoff of juices. Place chops on foil. Add beer, sauteed onion and butter. Sprinkle garlic salt on chops each time you turn them. Do not cook chops. When they are warm, remove foil from grill.

Antelope Curry

2 lbs. Antelope roast, steak of filet marinated till tender in buttermilk and tenderizer
1 can golden mushroom soup
1 soup can water
1 med. bell pepper, chopped
1 large onion, chopped
1 tbsp. Curry powder or to taste
2 tbsp. Bacon fat
1 tsp. Chili powder
Salt and pepper
1 tsp. MSG

Directions

Cut Antelope into bite-size chunks and salt and pepper to taste; then roll in flour to coat.

Put Mushroom Soup, water, bell pepper and onions in a pot and simmer until tender. Add water if necessary.

Add Antelope and seasonings to pot. Simmer until venision is warm (2 minutes) stirring to mix thoroughly. Serve immediately with Chutney and Rice. Do NOT overcook.

Quick Cooked Antelope

1-2 lbs. cubed Antelope, marinated in buttermilkwith tenderizer, then washed and cleaned
4-6 baby carrots
1-2 med. onion, chopped
1 diced celery stalk
2 ounces butter
1-2 tbsp. bacon fat
1/4-1/2 tsp. sage
1 tsp. Sugar
Flour to thicken
1 cup sherry or red wine

Directions

Barely Brown Antelope in butter. Add seasonings, celery, carrots, onion, carrots, and enough wine and water to cover meat. Cook until tender; thicken sauce with flour and add wine. Good with white or wild rice.

Antelope Tenderloin

1 Antelope tenderloin
2 tbsp. Bacon fat
1 tsp. black pepper
1 can Peaches
1 can Apricots
6 dried apricots
1 tbsp. Sugar
1/2 tsp. MSG

Directions

Preheat oven to 170 F.
Drain cans of Apricot and Peaches. Add dried Apricots and put fruit in a blender and blend on high. Add 1 tbsp. sugar and 1/2 tsp. MSG. Warm sauce.

Put Antelope in a pan. Cover with Bacon Fat and sprinkle with Salt and Pepper.

Place in the oven. Remove Antelope as soon as it is warm. Do NOT overcook' Cut into slices and cover with fruit sauce and serve.

Antelope Tid Bits

2 lbs. Antelope
1 tsp. thyme
One half tsp. tarragon
1/2 tsp. garlic powder
1 cup. diced onions
1 cup sliced mushrooms
4 oz. Bacon Fat
Salt and pepper to taste
Buttermilk

Directions

Cut Antelope into bite-size chunks. Then, marinate the Antelope for 3 hours in buttermilk. If it is an old animal add a little tenderizer. Wash Antelope thoroughly to remove buttermilk.

Heat oven to 170 F. Use 2 oz of bacon fat to coat the Antelope pieces.

Then heat in oven until the Antelope is warm.

Lightly saute the onion, mushrooms, thyme and garlic powder in the remaining bacon fat.

Slice the Antelope on a warm serving dish, top with sauteed onion/ mushroom mix and serve.

Antelope Sauteed

2-3 lbs. Antelope
1/2 cup olive oil
1/4 tsp. black pepper
1/3 cup Port Wine
3/4 tsp. Salt
1 large onion, chopped
1/4 tsp. garlic salt (or to taste)
1 tsp. sugar
1 tsp. oregano

Directions

Marinate the Antelope in buttermilk or yogurt for 3 hours to clean the taste. If meat is tough, add tenderizer. Then wash thoroughly.

Reserve ½ the oil foe sauteing. Then mix all ingredients together and remarinate the Antelope for 3 hours to flavor it.

Saute the Antelope quickly and very lightly. Sprinkle pepper. Slice and serve. If you like, boil down the wine marinade for a sauce oe serve with your favorit meat or barbecue sauce. Great for sandwiches.

Antelope Cassoulet

(This is longer than our usual Recipes but it will feed and army and can be frozen)

2-3 lbs. Cubed Antelope
I package Great Northern Beans
1 med. onion, diced
6-8 baby carrots
2 stalks celery, diced
3 tbsp. tomato paste
1 Quart stock
Salt and pepper
Garlic to taste
One tsp. Thyme
One half tsp.Tarragon
1 tbsp. Sugar
One Kielb.asa skinned and diced

Directions

Marinate Antelope cubes in buttermilk with one tsp. meat tenderizer

Soak beans in water overnight,

Drain Beans. Add all other ingredients to pot and simmer until tender.

Simmer until Antelope is tender. Correct seasonings and serve.

Antelope Pepper Steak

2 lbs. sliced meat marinated in bruuermilk then washed clean
Flour for dredging meat
Salt and ground red & black pepper to taste
2 medium chopped onion
1 box sliced mushrooms

Directions

Coat meat with flour after it has been salted and peppered. Brown quickly in moderately hot cooking oil. Cook covered until meat is pink in the center.

Remove meat from pan and make gravy by adding de glazing the pan with red wine or sherry.

Cook onion and muchrooms together separately and serve with the meat

Antelope Cassoulet

Chefs Note: This is longer than our usual Recipes but just as easy and it is delicious, easy to make and will feed an army

2 lb. Cubed Antelope
1 package Great Northern Beans
1 med. onion, diced
6 small carrots
2 stalks celery, diced
3 tbsp. tomato paste
1 Quart stock
Salt and pepper
Garlic to taste
One half tsp. Thyme
One half tsp.Tarragon
1 Kielb.asa skinned and diced

Directions

Marinate Antelope cubes in buttermilk wit one tsp. meat tenderizer overnight.

Soak beans in water overnight,

Drain Beans. Add all ingredients to pot and simmer until tender.

Simmer until Antelope is tender. Add water as necessary to prevent sticking to bottom of pan. Correct seasonings and serve.

Antelope Pepper Steak

2 lbs. sliced meat marinated in buttermilk then washed clean
Flour for dredging meat
Salt and ground Chili powswe to taste
2 medium chopped onion
1 box sliced mushrooms

Directions

Coat meat with flour after it has been salted and peppered. Brown outside quickly in moderately hot cooking oil. Remove meat from pan.

Saute onions and muchrooms together, separately fro meat and serve with the meat. Reserve and keep warm. Then make gravy by adding de glazing the pan with red wine or sherry.

Antelope Enchiladas

1 lb. ground Antelope
1 onion
Olive oil or bacon fat salt and pepper
1 tsp. garlic powder
1 tbsp. sugar
2 cans enchilada sauce
1 dozen corn tortillas
1/2 lb. sharp cheddar cheese, grated
6 black olives, chopped

Directions

Place Antelope and onion in skillet and saute in oil until meat is browned and onion cooked through. Stir in garlic, sugar, olives and salt and pepper to taste. Heat enchilada sauce in large round pan. Dip each tortilla in the hot sauce, remove almost at once and place on flat surface.

Spoon 1 tablespoon of meat mixture on tortilla, roll up, and place in greased 9x13 baking dish. Repeat with all tortillas and make single layer in dish, top with cheese.

Bake 15-20 minutes at 375 degrees F.

Baked Antelope Steak

1 lb. Antelope round steak sliced and marinated in Buttermilk and tenderizer then washed clean
1 tsp. Salt
1 diced onion
1 tsp. pPepper
One half box sliced musrooms
1 tbsp. flour
1 minced garlic clove
1 green bell pepper
1 tbsp. bacon fat or olive oil
1 cup red wine of sherry

Directions

Salt and pepper 8-10 pieces of Antelope steak and roll in flour. Place in baking container and saute in hot oil until brown. Add all other ingredients and stir. Bake in 300 oven for 45 minutes. Add water as needed. Correct seasonings.

Grilled Antelope Steak

Marinate 4 (1/2" thick) Antelope steaks in buttermilk and meat tenderizer for 24 hours. Then wash thoroughly.
Enough dry Mustard to coat meat

1 tbsp. pepper
2 tbsp. olive oil
1/4 cup margarine
Dash salt

Directions

This only works on an outdoor grill. Brush Antelope steaks (from leg, rib, or loin chops of young animal) with olive oil. Coat the Steaks with dry mustard and pepper. Grill the steaks until done to taste. Combine margarine and salt and brush on broiled steaks.

Stuffed Antelope Steak

1 lb. round Antelope steak cut thin
1/2 tsp. Each Salt and Pepper
1/2 tsp. Garlic powder
1 egg
1/2 cup milk or broth
1 medium diced onion
1 cup Stuffing Mix
1 tbsp. flour
1/2 cup sherry
2 tbsp. bacon fat

Directions

Marinate round steak in buttermilk and tenderizer

Mix bread crumbs, milk, sherry, egg, and seasonings to make stuffing.

Salt the meat and cut into 2" x 4" pieces. Spread each piece or meat with dressing and roll, fastening the rolls with toothpicks. Roll in flour and brown in fat. Place in pan, add, cover and cook for 1 hr. at 300 degrees.

Antelope Steak au Poire

Cut steaks thin and marinate Steaks in Buttermilk AND tenderizer.

2 lbs. Antelope steak
2 tbsp. Olive oil
Salt and fresh ground pepper garlic powder to taste
1 cup sour cream
2 tbsp. sherry

Directions

Wash steaks thoroughly, Sprinkle salt and cover with pepper steaks and saute in olive oil. When nicely brown, remove from pan and reserve. Add garlic and sherry to deglaze pan. Add sour cream over cutlets and stir to make a sauce.

Pour sauce over steaks and serve. Serves 6-8.

If you do NOT add tenderizer, simply warm steaks. Do NOT cook

Sauteed Filet of Antelope

Wash Antelope thoroughly.
Cut filet into 3/4" to 1" thick slices butter
Frozen lemonade (easier)

Directions

Brush sliced fillet with a very small amount of lemonade. let standfo 115 minutes. If using lemon slices, alternate the slices of Antelope and lemon, put in refrigerator; wait 15-30 minutes. Remove, turn over, and rebrush with lemonad. Again, let stand in refrigerator 15-30 minutes.

Warm filets in skillet but do NOT cook. Turn cook until rare. Sprinkle with salt and serve. Serve rare. Do not overcook as Antelope is dry and will toughen almost immediately.

Easy Barbecued Antelope

2 lbs. Antelope
Your favorite barbecue sauce
1 tsp. Garlic Powder
1 quart Antelope or beef stock
1/2 cup port wine

Directions

Mix Garlic powder and port wine into barbecue Sauce

Cook Antelope in stock until well done. Cool. Remove meat from bones and cut up. Save and freeze Stock!

Put meat on a serving dish. Pour barbecue sauce mix over meat and put in oven to heat. This is a good way to use the bony parts of a deer.

Antelope Strogonoff

2 lbs. Antelope roast, steak of filet marinated in buttermilk and tenderizer
4 tbsp. Bacon fat
1 large onion, chopped
Flour to coat meat
Salt and pepper
One half pt. sour cream
One cup bechamel (White) sauce*
1 tsp. garlic powder
4 tbsp. Flour
1 tsp. MSG

Directions

Mix butter and flour in a double boiler. Slowly ad milk and seasonings, stirring to blend

Cut Antelope into bite-size chunks, salt and pepper to taste, roll in flour to coat. Heat bacon fat to hot, saute Antelope quickly, remove from pan.

Add pepper and onions and cook until tender. Drain off bacon fat. Add sour cream. Return Antelope to pan. Stir to mix thoroughly; cover with a lid and simmer until tender. Serve over rice.

Antelope Roast

4 lb. Antelope Round
4-6 slices of bacon
1 tsp. Salt
One half tsp. pepper
1 quart meat stock
2 tsp. garlic powder six small carrots
1 pkg mushrooms
1 medium onion one half cup minced celery
1 cup Port wine

Directions

Saute 6 slices of bacon (crisp) in Dutch oven. Remove bacon and leave grease in oven. Sprinkle roast with garlic powder, salt and pepper. Heat bacon grease and sear roast on all sides until brown. Add diced diced onion, carrots, mushrooms and celery. Cook very slowly for about 3 hours (or until done). Blend vegetables to thicken sauce. Add Port Wine and serve.

Antelope Steaks in Sherry Sauce

4 Antelope T-bone or loin steaks, cut about 1/2 inch thick
1/2 cup sherry
3 Tbsp. butter salt and pepper
1 tbsp. chopped chives
2 tbsp. Blackberry or currant jelly
1/8 tsp.nutmeg
1 tsp. sugar

Directions

Trim any excess fat from steaks. Sprinkle steaks with salt, pepper and sugar then saute steaks in a 10-inch pan over medium heat, in warm butter—about 1 or 2 minutes on each side until warm.

Remove from heat and place on warm platter.

Pour off fat. Deglaze pan with sherry. Mix with nutmeg, chives and Blackberry jelly/jam. Pour sauce over steaks and serve.

Antelope Soup

1 1/2 pounds Antelope diced into 1/2-3/4 inch pieces
2 quarts water
1 quart can Chicken stock
I large diced onion.
12 baby carrots
1 cup chopped celery
Salt to taste
2 tsp. Chili Powder
1 tbsp. Sugar
2 tbsp. Bacon fat
1 can sweet corn
1 tsp. Garlic powder
2 tsp. MSG

Directions

In a big pot, saute onions until brown. Drain the corn and add the remainder of ingredients. Cover with water and stock. Simmer on low for two hours or until meat is tender.

Correct the seasonings and serve. You can either freeze the soup or store it in the frig.

Easy Antelope Soup

1 1/2 pound Antelope cut into 1/2-3/4 inch pieces.
1 pkg. Onion soup mix
1 cans golden mushroom soup
1 tbsp. Frozen orange juice
1 tsp. msg
1 can Italian style stewed tomatoes
1 tbsp. Chili Powder

Directions

Saute Antelope until brown in the bottom of your pot. Add remaining ingredients with water and simmer until tender. Add water as needed.

Correct seasonings and serve.

Antelope Vegetable Pot

Neck or backbone broken in chunks, fat removed
1 chopped onion
1 tsp. garlic powder
2 cups Meat stock
2 tsp. salt
1 tsp. Chile Powder
One half cup all purpose flour
10 baby carrots
1 cup lima beans
1 can corn drained
2 med. potatoes cooked and diced
1/2 cup all purpose flour
1 cup sherry
1/2 cup cream
3 ribs of celery, chopped salt and pepper to taste

Directions

Thoroughly clean and wash Antelope. Place Antelope, stock, onion, garlic, carrots, celery, salt and pepper in pot; cover and boil. Reduce heat and simmer for 2 hours. Add water as needed. Remove bones from pot, pick meat, and dice.

Add cream, potatoes, corn and lima beans to pot. Correct seasonings, add brandy or sherry, cover and bake at 350 degrees for 20 minutes and serve.

Strain some broth and blender with flour. Add to pot with cream, potatoes, corn and lima beans. Correct seasonings, add brandy or sherry, cover and bake at 350 degrees for 20 minutes and serve.

Antelope Crown Roast

1 rack of Antelope
Salt pork for larding
Freshly ground black pepper
4 to 5 tbsp. butter, melted

Directions

It is easy to prepare the meat. The backbone must be cut with a saw between each rib portion enough so the ribs can be bent and then tied into a crown,

The rib bones are left rather long so they curve dramatically outwardly as the meat section is turned to the center. You then want to remove the fat and place bacon over the chops.

Preheat oven to 450 F. Place in roasting pan, coat with the butter and sprinkle with pepper. Roast for 15 minutes. Lower heat to 350 F. and continue to roast 12 to 15 minutes per pound—NO LONGER. Baste occasionally.

While the Antelope is roasting begin to prepare a Cumberland Sauce.

There is an excellent on in the Joy of Cooking or you can use this as well. Mix:

1-1/2 cups red wine
1 half cup brown sugar
1 quarter tsp. cloves
1 quarter tsp. ginger
1 quarter tsp. Pepper
1 cup Currant of Blackberry Jelly
1 tsp. thyme
Salt

Antelope Stock

Thoroughly clean and wash Antelope
Antelope
Water to cover
2 Large chopped Onions
Garlic Powder
Salt and Pepper
2 tsp. sugar
1 tsp. MSG
2 tbsp. butter or bacon fat

Directions

Marinate Antelope in buttermilk and themn wash to remove gamey taste.

Cut off all fat. Boil meat, onions and seasonings in water to cover until it falls off bone;

Remove meat and cut it into small pieces. Put in frying pan with butter or bacon fat and saute until slightly brown. Correct all seasonings. Save the meat for hash. Use the stock for gravies or freeze.

Ginger Antelope

2 lbs. cubed Antelope roast or steak
2 chopped onions
1 1/2 tsp. salt
1 tsp. Chili Powder
1 can stewed Italian tomatoes
1 tsp. turmeric
1 tsp. cumin
1/2 cup oil
1 tbsp. sugar
2 tsp. Garlic Powder
4 tsp. powdered ginger
1 can onion soup

Directions

Combine onions, turmeric, ginger, salt, and meat. Let stand 1 hour. Saute lightly in large frying pan. Add tomatoes, seasonings and onion soup; cover and simmer 1 1/2 hours adding water (or Port wine) if the mixture gets too dry. Serve over rice.

Antelope Roast in Sour Cream

3 lbs. Antelope roast. Then marinate overnight in buttermilk with meat tenderizer if this is an old animal and wash thoroughly
3 tbsp. olive oil or bacon fat
1 pint sour cream
1 Pint meat stock
1 pint Port Wine
2 onions diced
Garlic Powder to taste
1 tsp. Powdered sage, 2 tsp. Leaf sage
1 tsp. Each Chili Powder and Salt
2 tsp. Each of Chili Powder and Salt
1/2 tsp. MSG

Directions

Brown the roast and the onions in the pot. Add stock and seasonings and roast till tender. At the end, add the sour cream but so not boil.

Antelope Roast in Sherry

Wash one Antelope roast thoroughly
One pkg. dry onion soup mix
I tsp. garlic
1 cup sherry wine
1 tbsp. sugar

Directions

Preheat oven to 425 degrees then reduce the heat to 350 degrees. Place roast on a large piece of heavy duty aluminum foil. Sprinkle 1/2 pkg. of dry onion soup over meat. Wrap the Antelope in the foil and seal the edges tightly.
Place the wrapped meat in a baking pan and roast for 2 to 2 1/2 hours or until tender. Remove the roast and put it on a pleat. Pour off any fat from the juices. Add red wine sage, sugar and juices and thicken with flour or corn starch to make a gravy. (Tip: use corn starch if you want a lighter gravy

Antelope Roast in Sherry

Wash one Antelope roast thoroughly
1 2-4 LB. Antelope Roast
One pkg. dry onion soup mix
I tsp. garlic
1 tsp. Chili Powder
2 tsp. Sage
1 cup sherry wine
1 tbsp. sugar

Directions

Preheat the oven to 350 degrees. Place roast on a large piece of heavy duty aluminum foil. Sprinkle Chili Powder, Sage and 1/2 pkg. of dry onion soup over meat. Wrap the Antelope in the foil and seal the edges tightly.

Place the wrapped meat in a baking pan and roast for 2 to 2 1/2 hours or until tender. Remove the roast and put it on a pleat. Pour off any fat from the juices. Add the Sherry wine sage, sugar and juices and thicken with flour or corn starch to make a gravy. (Tip: use corn starch if you want a lighter gravy

Mexican Antelope Stew

Serves 5
3 lbs. Antelope, cut into 1" cubes
1 pound bite size Chirozo sausages
2 cans red beans
1 large can tomatoes
3 medium onions, diced 1"
15 Baby Carrots
3 stalks celery, diced 1"
2 tsp. Garlic Powder
2 tbsp. chili powder
1/4 cup flour, all purpose
2 cups red wine
2 cups meat stock
1 teaspoon salt
1/2 tsp. ground thyme

Directions

Brown venison and sausage in a large pot, add all vegetable except beans and sauté for 5 more minutes. Then add the beef stock and cook for 3 minutes. Then add red wine and seasonings.

Let simmer 1 hour and serve with hot French bread. IMPORTANT—stir occasiionally so the stew does not stick to the bottom of the pot and burn. At the end Blend vegetables on high to thicken sauce. Add the Beans and simmer 3 minutes longer. Serves 10.

Elegant Antelope Stew

2 lbs. Antelope steak
1/2 lb. Bacon or salt pork
2 tbsp. flour
6 cups of stock
1 can Italian stewed tomatoes or preferably zucchini
8 baby carrots
2 Stalks diced celery diced
1 tbsp. sugar
7 small onions
Garlic Powder to taste
1 cup peas
Salt and pepper to taste

Directions

Cut bacon into 1" cubes and saute in large saucepan until lightly browned.

Remove and set aside. Cut Antelope into 1 1/2 or 2" pieces and brown over high heat in bacon fat. Stir in flour and make a roux. Lower heat and let brown 2-3 minutes. Then add stock and stir till smooth. Simmer 1 hour or more until Antelope begins to get tender, add more liquid as necessary.

Add all the other ingredients, except peas, and continue to simmer to make a thick stew. Simmer peas in a separate pan until done. Strain and spoon over or around stew when served. Serve with corn muffins, potatoes or parsnips and a salad.

Irish Antelope Stew

Cut Antelope into chunks and marinate Antelope in buttermilk to clean taste and tenderize the meat.
2 pounds of your a chosen, (Antelope, Buffalo, Elk, Beef, Antleope, Lamb)
1 tsp. Dry M ustard
1 tablespoon black peppercorns
3 garlic cloves, coarsely chopped
1-1/2 cups Port wine
2 to 3 tbsp. olive oil
2 cups celery pieces
1 can small boiling onions
1 cups beef stock salt and pepper to tasrw

Directions

Wash buttermilk off the Antelope. Mix the meat, juniper berries, peppercorns and garlic. Add 1 cup of the red wine. Cover and marinate in the refrigerator for 2 to 3 hours, or overnight.

Drain off the marinade and save. Heat the olive oil in your pot and brown the Antelope. Add the celery and onions. Add all the red wine and 3/4 cup beef stock. Cover and bake in a preheated 350°F oven for 45 minutes, or until tender, adding the remaining beef stock during baking if necessary.

Remove from the oven. Season with salt and pepper and serve. Garnish serving plate with shamrocks and have a happy St. Patrick's day!

Italian Antelope Stew

Marinte Antelope in yogurt or buttermilk. Then wash thoroughly
2 lbs. stew meat
1 can Zucchini
1 cup chopped celery
2 tbsp. olive oil or bacon fat
1 diced medium onion
2 tsp. Garlic powder
1 tsp. salt
1 tbsp. Sugar
1/2 tsp. Pepper
2 cups Port wine
2 tsp. Powdered Oregano

Directions

Brown the cubed meat in the oil, add two cups of water, then the rest of the ingredients. Cover and simmer 1 1/2 hours. Remove bay leaves, add carrots and potatoes, cook another 30-45 minutes or until tender. As a footnote, I've just browned the meat, then dumped everything in the "crockpot" on low. It produces a stew that tastes as tho' it already been reheated several times.

Basic Antelope Stew

Marinte Antelope in buttermilk. Then wash thoroughly
2 lbs. stew meat
12 baby carrots
6 potatoes
2 tbsp. Oil or Bacon Fat
1 tsp. Worcestershire sauce
1 medium onion
1 tsp. salt
2 tsp. Sugar
1/2 tsp. Pepper
1 tsp. Garlic powder
1 1/2 tsp. sage
3 cups Port Wine

Directions

Brown the cubed meat in the oil, add wine, then the rest of the ingredients.

Cover and simmer 1 1/2 hours. Add carrots and potatoes, cook another 30-45 minutes or until tender.

Check frequently to correct seasonings and add more water or wine as needed.

If you have a crockpot, use that to simmer. Check fluids, correct seasoning and serve.

Antelope Stew with Rosemary

3 lbs. boneless Antelope cut into bite sized portions
1 tbsp. sugar
2 large diced onions
Flour
1 tsp. garlic powder
Salt and pepper to taste
3 tbsp. bacon fat
2 tsp. Rosemary
2 cups meat stock

Directions

Marinate Antelope in buttermilk or yogurt overnight to soften meat and clean taste. Wash thoroughly, dust with flour, salt, and pepper.

Brown meat on all sides in bacon fat over medium heat; add onions and remaining ingredients. Cover and simmer approximately 1 1/4 hours or until tender.

Antelope Sausage

Mexican Antelope Sausage

5 lbs. Antelope, coarse ground
1 lb. Bacon fat
2 tbsp. monosodium glutamate
1 tsp. jalapeno pepper
2 tbsp. salt
2 tbsp. Sugar
2 large onions processed to liquid
3 green peppers
2 tbsp. Chili Powder
1 tbsp. ground sage
1 tbsp. garlic powder

Directions

Grind or process meat, onion and bacon fat. Mix seasonings thoroughly with Antelope and re-grind or reprocess. Cook a small sample to test flavor. Adapt spices to taste. Wine may be used to moisten the mixture if it is to be stuffed in casings. Keeps well about 1 year in freezer.

Smoked Antelope Sausage

4 lbs. meat, 1/2 Antelope, 1/2 pork
1 cup Bacon Fat
1 tbsp. garlic powder
1 large onion cut fine
1/2 cup salt
1 1/2 tbsp. Chili Powder
3 tbsp. ground sage
1 cup Hickory Flavored Barbecue sauce
1 cup sugar
1 tsp. MSG
1 cup oatmeal (for binder)
1/2 cup water

Directions

Clean, wash and grind your Antelope. Then mix with herbs, salt, msg, Chili Powder, sugar, water, Barbecue Sauce, oatmeal and water.

Mix thoroughly in a food processor. Pack meat in containers sausage casings. The meat may be stored in a freezer and used as you would good pork sausage.

Classic Antelope Sausage

2 pounds ground Antelope from tough cuts like shoulder, flank, or neck
1 pound pork loin and/or shoulder
1 1/2 cups bacon fat
3 tbsp. salt
1 tablespoon ground black pepper
2 tbsp. powdered garlic
1 tbsp. powdered onion
1 tbsp. ground cumin
3 tbsp. ground sage
5-9 tbsp. sugar
4 tbsp. instant oatmeal
1 tbsp. msg. (accent)

Directions

Grind The Antelope and Pork together

Add all ingredients and mix well. Add water if mix is too dry. Freeze the mix in plastic containers. Unfreeze, make into portion size pieces and saute and serve needed. Refreeze the rest of the sausage to use on the next occasion.

Spicey Antelope Sausage

5 lbs. Antelope, coarse ground
2 cups bacon fat
1 tbsp. monosodium glutamate
1 tsp. jalapeno pepper
3 tbsp. salt
3 tbsp. sugar
2 tbsp. garlic powder
3 red bell peppers
3 tbsp. Chili Powder
Red wine
1 tbsp. ground sage

Directions

Process ground Antelope and bacon fat together. Spread on a clean surface and sprinkle evenly with seasonings, mix thoroughly and re-grind if necessary. Test hotness by sauteing a small sample. Adjust seasonings. If the mix is too mild add seasonings. If too salty or too hot add more meat.

Wine may be used to moisten the mixture. Store in containers covering the meat with plastic wrap to avoid dehydration.

Keeps well about 1 year in freezer.

Italian Antelope Sausage

4 lbs. Antelope, coarse ground
12 ounces bacon fat
1 tbsp. monosodium glutamate
2 tbsp. ground Oregano
3 tbsp. salt
5 tbsp. black pepper
5 tbsp. sugar
2 tbsp. garlic powder
2 finely chopped onions
3 tbsp. Parmesan cheece

Directions

Process ground Antelope and bacon fat together. Spread on a clean surface and sprinkle evenly with seasonings, mix thoroughly and re-grind if necessary.

Test hotness by sauteing a small sample. Adjust seasonings. If the mix is too mild add seasonings. If too salty or too hot add more meat. Wine may be used to moisten the mixture. Store in containers covering the meat with plastic wrap to avoid dehydration.

Keeps well about 1 year when frozen.

Herbed Antelope Sausage

5 lbs. Antelope, coarse ground
2 cups bacon fat
1 tbsp. monosodium glutamate
2 tbsp. Ground Cinnamon
1 tbsp. Ground Nutmeg
3 tbsp. Salt
1/2 tsp. Ground clovest
1 1/2 tbsp. Chili Powder
5 tbsp. sugar
2 tbsp. garlic powder
3 finely chopped green bell peppers
1 tbsp. MSG

Directions

Process ground Antelope and bacon fat together. Spread on a clean surface and sprinkle evenly with seasonings, mix thoroughly and re-grind if necessary. Test hotness by sauteing a small sample. Adjust seasonings. If the mix is too mild add seasonings. If too salty or too hot add more meat.

Wine may be used to moisten the mixture. Store in containers covering the meat with plastic wrap to avoid dehydration.

Keeps well about 1 year in freezer.

TexMex Antelope Sausage

3 lbs. Antelope, Hamburger
2 lbs. Pork Hamburger
1 Pint Bacon Fat
1 cup smoke flavored Barbecue Sauce
3 tbsp. Chili Powder
3 tbsp. Paprika
1 1/2 tbsp. garlic powder
1 tsp. crushed Jalapeno pepper, to taste
1/4 cup salt
1/4 cup Sugar

Directions

Mix all ingredients and grind several times. sausage may be frozen without smoking in patties, sausage bags, or casings.

Sweet Antelope Sausage

5 lbs. Ground Antelope
2 tbsp. MSG
6 tbsp. sugar
1 1/2 tbsp. black pepper
1 tbsp.Allspice
1 1/2 tbsp. garlic powder
1 tbsp. coriander
1/4 cup salt

Directions

Mix all ingredients and gtind several times diced Antelope. This sausage may be frozen without smoking and made in patties, hors d'oeuvre balls sausage bags, or put into casings.

Antelope Cornmeal Meatloaf

1 1/2 lb. Ground Antelope
2/3 cup corn meal
1 1/2 cup water
1 tbsp. Flour
2 tsp. Garlic
2 tbsp. bacon fat
1 small chopped onion
2 tsp. Salt
1 tsp. Chili Powder
1 tbsp. sugar
2 eggs

Directions

Mix cornmeal, eggs and water in bowl. Brown Antelope and onion in bacon fat;

Add salt, chili and garlic powder, and cornmeal mixture. Stir continuallyl and cook 15 minutes. Place in greased loaf pan and bake 35-40 minutes at 350 degrees.

Serve Plain or with your favorite Pasta Sauce.

Antelope Meatloaf

2 lbs. ground Antelope
1/2 lb. ground beef
3 tbsp. butter or margarine
1 cup minced onion
1/4 cup minced celery
2 eggs
1 cup quick oatmeal
1 cup sherry or port wine
1 tbsp. Each salt and pepper
1 tbsp. sugar
2 tsp. garlic powder
2 tsp. Powdered Thyme leaves
1 tsp. Cinamon

Directions

Preaheat oven to 350 degrees. Saute onions and celery until tender, about 5 minutes. Mix oatmeal, eggs, and then all other ingredients except meat in a large bowl. Add Antelope, beef and onion mixture; mix again.

Place mixture in 9x5" loaf pan and bake 1 1/2 hours. Pour off pan juices. Serve hot or cold with your favorite pasta sauce. Makes 8 to 10 servings.

Antelope and Bacon Meatloaf

2 pounds ground Antelope
One cup ground pork
1 cup minced onion
1 cup bacon fat
1/2 cup minced onion
1/4 cup minced celery
2 eggs
1 cup fresh bread crumbs
1/2 cup milk
2 tsp. Each salt and pepper
1 tsp. thyme leaves
2 tbsp. sugar
3 Bacon slices
1 tsp. Garlic Powder

Directions

Preheat oven to 350 degrees. Beat eggs with a fork. Thoroughly mix eggs and all other ingredients together in a large bowl. Place mixture in loaf pan or pans cover tops with sliced bacon.

Bake 1 hours. Pour off pan juices. Cover with you favorite heated spaghetti sauce and serve.

Antelope Hash

3 tbsp. Bacon drippings
1 large Onion, chopped
3 cups Cooked and ground Antelope leftovers.
2 Med. potatoes cut in 16 pcs.
1 tbsp. Flour
1 clove minced Garlic
2 cups Beef broth
1/4 tsp. Black pepper
2 tsp. salt
1/4 tsp. thyme
2 tsp. Chili powder

Directions

Brown onion and potatoes in bacon fat. Remove vegetables, add flour and mix with fat to make a roux. Replace veggies in pan, add Antelope, broth and other ingredients. Let simmer until tender.

Antelope Sloppy Joe's Mix lbs. Antelope hamburger

1 cups of chopped onion
1/2 cup bacon fat
1 1/2 cups Pasta Sauce (your Choice)
1 cups water
1 tbsp. Garlic powder
1 tsp. Salt
1 cup chopped green pepper
1 tbsp. Sugar
2 tsp. Chili Powder

Directions

Saute onions and Antelope brown in bacon fat. Add all other ingredients; mix thoroughly; bring to a boil and simmer 5 minutes. Pour into sterile clean Mason pint jars almost to the top. Put on the lids and freeze (safest) or boil the jars again completely covered by water fo 15 minutes. DO NOT OPEN JARS IF THE CENTER OF THE LIDS HAS POPPED UP! THROW AWAY!

Antelope with Pasta Roni

3 lbs. ground Antelope
1 cup chopped onion
1 tsp. Garlic powder
1/4 cup salad oil
2 jars of Pasta sauce
1/2 tsp. pepper
2 tsp. salt for sauce
2 tsp. oregano
2 tbsp. salt for macaroni
1 lb. macaroni product
2 cups cottage cheese
1 lb. Mozzarella cheese, sliced thin
1/2 cup grated Parmesan cheese

Directions

This is a good berlly stuffer. Lightly saute ground Antelope and onion until meat is evenly browned. Add spaghetti sauce and spices. Simmer, stirring occasionally, about 10-15 minutes. Do not allow the sauce to dry out and stick bottom of the pot.

Cook macaroni in salted water, Drain and add cottage cheese. Layer 1/3 of the meat sauce on the bottom of a baking pan. Then add half the macaroni and cheese mix. The another layer of meat and more of the macaroni cheexze mix and a final layer meat.

Cover the top with a thin layer of parmesan cheese. Arrange black olives or canned artichoke hearts on top to decorate and bake at 350 degrees F. 20-30 minutes until bubbly. Cut into serving size pieces and serve with a spatula.

Antelope Meat Balls

1 and one half lbs. ground Antelope
1 cup cooked quick oat meal
1 tsp. Each salt and pepper
2/3 cup onion, finely chopped
One half tsp. sage
Garlic powder (to taste)
1/4 cup bacon fat
1 tbsp. flour
1 cup milk
1/4 tsp. cinnamon, ginger and nutmeg
1 tsp. sugar

Directions

Combine oatmeal, Antelope, salt, pepper, onion, sage and garlic powder; shape into balls about 1" in diameter. Brown meatballs in bacon fat, cover pan; cook over low heat 15 minutes. Remove meatballs from pan and add flour to drippings. Add milk, sugar, cinnamon, nutmeg and ginger to make gravy and simmer 3-4 minutes (without boiling). Serve gravy hot over the meat balls.

Antelope Rice Meat Balls

1 lb. ground Antelope
1 cup parmesan cheese
1 tbsp. sugar
1 tsp. garlic powder
1 cup cooked rice
1/4 cup bacon fat
1 chopped onion
1/3 tsp. cinnamon
1/3 tsp. nutmeg salt and pepper
1 jar spaghetti sauce

Directions

Mix meat, rice, onion, sugar, parmesan and seasonings. Make into balls and saute until brown in bacon fat. Pour sauce over the mixture and bake 1 1/2 hrs. at 325 degrees. Add water as needed

Antelope Rosemary Meat Loaf

2 lbs. ground Antelope
1/4 tbsp. Chili Powder
1/2 cup bacon fat
1 tbsp. salt
1 tsp. pepper
1 tsp. Garlic powder
1 lb. ground pork
1 jar Pasta sauce
1 cup milk
1/2 cup quick oats
1 egg
1 chopped med. Onion
2 tsp. Rosemary
1 tsp. MSG

Directions

Mix all ingredients except the Pasta sauce. Place in a loaf pan Bake at 350 degrees for 1 hour. Pour off fat, Cover with spaghetti sauce and serve

Antelope Hamburgers

Antelope is a Dry and Tough meat so for best results, you should add fat, preferably Bacon Fat to all Antelope Hamburgers

Antelope Hamburger

5 lbs. lean Antelope
2 tbsp. sage
1-1 1/2 cups bacon fat
1 tbsp. salt
1 tbsp. liquid smoke
5 tbsp. sugar
2 tbsp. pepper

Grind and thoroughly mix all ingredients, form into patties and pan fry. Wrap individually in butter fat and it will keeps for 1 year in the freezer.

German Style Antelope Hamburger

2 lbs. Ground Antelope
1 Knockwurst, skinned and diced
Salt and pepper
4 ounces Bacon fat
1 egg
1 small onion
1 tsp. Dill garlic powder to taste
3 ounces of Beer

Mix sausage and ground Antelope. Combine with remaining ingredients.

Brown until almost done. Add beer to deglaze the pan and make a sauce.

Polish Style Antelope Hamburger

2 lbs. Ground Antelope
1 Kielb.asa, skinned and diced
Salt and pepper
4 ounces Bacon fat
1 egg
1 small onion
1 tsp. Dill garlic powder to taste
3 ounces of Beer

Directions

Mix sausage and ground Antelope. Combine with remaining ingredients.
Brown until almost done. Add beer to deglaze the pan and make a sauce.

French Style Antelope Hamburger

2 lbs. Ground Antelope
1/4 lb. Brie Cheese
Salt and pepper
4 ounces Bacon fat
1 egg
1 small onion
1 tsp. Thyme garlic powder to taste
3 ounces of Red Wine

Directions

Mix sausage and ground Antelope. Combine with remaining ingredients.

Brown until almost done. Add wine to deglaze the pan and make a sauce.

Italian Style Antelope Hamburger

2 lbs. Ground Antelope
1/4 lb. Gorgonzola Cheese
Salt and pepper
4 ounces Bacon fat
1 egg
1 small onion
1 tsp. Oregano garlic powder to taste
3 ounces of Red Wine

Mix sausage and ground Antelope. Combine with remaining ingredients.
Brown until almost done. Ad d wine to deglaze the pan and make a sauce.

Danish Style Antelope Hamburger

2 lbs. Ground Antelope
1/4 lb. Danish Blue Cheese
Salt and pepper
4 ounces Bacon fat
1 egg
1 small onion
1 tsp. Thyme garlic powder to taste
3 ounces of Beer

Mix sausage and ground Antelope. Combine with remaining ingredients.

Brown until almost done. Add beer to deglaze the pan and make a sauce

Irish Style Antelope Hamburger

2 lbs. Ground Antelope
1/4 lb. Cheddar Cheese
Salt and pepper
4 ounces Bacon fat
1 egg
1 small onion
1 tsp. Thyme garlic powder to taste
3 ounces of Stout

Mix sausage and ground Antelope. Combine with remaining ingredients.

Brown until almost done. Add stout to deglaze the pan and make a sauce

English Style Antelope Hamburger

2 lbs. Ground Antelope
1/4 lb. Cheddar Cheese
Salt and pepper
4 ounces Bacon fat
1 egg
1 small onion
1 tsp. Thyme garlic powder to taste
3 ounces of Scotch Whiskey

Mix sausage and ground Antelope. Combine with remaining ingredients.

Brown until almost done. Add Whiskey to deglaze the pan and make a sauce

Mexican Style Antelope Hamburger

2 lbs. Ground Antelope
1/4 lb. Jalapeno Pepper Cheese
1 tbsp.Salt
4 ounces Bacon fat
1 egg
1 small onion
1 tbsp. Chili Powder garlic powder to taste
3 ounces of Corona Beer

Mix sausage and ground Antelope. Combine with remaining ingredients.

Brown until almost done. Add beer to deglaze the pan and make a sauce

American Style Antelope Hamburger

2 lbs. Ground Antelope
1/4 lb. Monterey Jack Cheese
Salt and pepper
4 ounces Bacon fat
1 egg
1 small onion
1 tbsp. Chili Powder garlic powder to taste
3 ounces of Bourbon Whiskey

Mix sausage and ground Antelope. Combine with remaining ingredients.

Brown until almost done. Add Whiskey to deglaze the pan and make a sauce

ARMADILLO RECIPES

Important—Read This First:

Chef Gahagan says, always marinate meat in Buttermilk and Meat Tenderizer for about three hours. Then wash off the buttermilk and remarinate in wine and herbs if desired.

Baked or Barbecued Armadillo

INGREDIENTS

Two lbs. armadillo meat
8 ounces of butter
Lemon juice
Salt to taste
Pepper/lemon pepper to taste

DIRECTIONS

Season with salt, pepper, lemon pepper, lemon juice, and rub with butter.

Wrap in foil and bake at 325 degrees F. for approximately 45 minutes. Remove foil, add more butter and brown. For barbecued armadillo, baste with barbecue sauce over grill after removing foil.

Armadillo with Mustard Sauce

INGREDIENTS

Two lbs. armadillo meat
One 1/4 cups dry white wine
1/2 cup oil
1/2 tsp. garlic powder
Salt and pepper to taste
1 tsp. mustard or to taste
1 med. onion, sliced thin
1 1/4 cups light cream
1 tbsp. cornstarch

DIRECTIONS

Mix all ingredients of marinade and add armadillo. Marinate about 8 hrs., turning meat occasionally. Remove armadillo and reserve marinade.

Melt butter in deep skillet and brown armadillo pieces. Pour in marinade and bring to a boil. Stir in seasoning, cover and simmer until tender (about 1-1 1/4 hours.) Remove skillet from the fire and place armadillo pieces on a warmed platter.

Mix mustard and cornstarch, then mix in cream. Return skillet to low heat and stir in this mixture a little at a time. Stir sauce until hot, but not boiling, and thickened. Pour sauce over armadillo. Serve with steamed rice.

Armadillo With Rice

INGREDIENTS

1 armadillo, dressed and cleaned
4 large onions
1 stalk celery
2 cans chopped mushrooms
2 cups rice, uncooked
Salt and pepper to taste
10 cups armadillo broth

DIRECTIONS

Saute onions in pot until golden. Add celery and boil armadillo with vegetables until tender; reserve broth. Remove meat from bones. Add mushrooms and meat and simmer for 5 minutes.

Put in a large baking pan or Dutch oven and add 10 cups of hot broth; add rice, salt and pepper; stir. Place in 375 degrees F. oven and cook until tender. Serves 12.

BEAR RECIPES

Chef's Note: Bear is a very rich meat and Young bear can be cooked like this. Steak from older bears should be made into stew.

Important—Read This First:

Marinate in buttermilk to clean taste. Wash thoroughly in water. Remarinate in red wine, water, 1 tbsp. sugar, salt and meat tenderizer.

Braised Bear Steak

Bear steak, 1" thick
Salt and pepper
1/2 tsp. Garlic powder or to taste
1 cup sliced onions
3 tbsp. bacon fat salt and pepper
One half package sliced mushrooms

Brown the onions and the mushrooms in the bacon fat. Grill meat or remove the onions and mushrooms from the pan and sauté the meat until tender.

Deglaze pan with red wine or Irish Cream for a sauce.

Surround with boiled (new) potatoes, honey covered carrots and parsley.

Serve with sautéed mushrooms.

Sauteed Fillet of Bear

INGREDIENTS

1 Bear Fillet
Salt and pepper
1/2 tsp. Garlic powder or to taste
3 tbsp. bacon fat
Salt and pepper

DIRECTIONS

Mix seasonings and rub into Fillet

Cut fillet into slices. Melt bacon fat and saute (pan fry) slices rare or medium rare over a medium heat. Do NOT overcook.

Roast Fillet of Bear

INGREDIENTS

1 Bear Fillet
Salt and pepper
1/2 tsp. Garlic powder or to taste
3 tbsp. bacon fat
Salt and pepper
1 box sliced mushrooms i thing sliced onion

DIRECTIONS

Mix seasonings and rub into Fillet

Saute onions and mushrooms until done. Remove to a plate.

Deglaze the pan and pour the remaining bscon fast into a roating pan. Roast until internal temperature (meat thermoneter) reaches 140 F. Remove from the oven, cover with sliced mushrooms and onions and serve with red wine. Do NOT iovercook.

Fine Cut Bear Steak

INGREDIENTS

1-2 lbs. bear steak
1 1/2 tbsp. vegetable oil
2 large onions, cut into 1/2" slices, rings
1 can (10 3/4 oz.) condensed cream of mushroom soup
1 (4 oz.) can sliced mushrooms drain & reserve liquid
1/2 cup sherry
1 1/2 tsp. garlic salt
3 cups hot cooked rice

DIRECTIONS

Cut steak into thin strips. In a large skillet (oven-proof, if desired), brown meat in oil, using high heat. Add onions.

Saute steak pieces until tender crisp. Blend soup, sherry, liquid from mushrooms, and garlic salt. Pour over steak. Add mushrooms. Reduce heat; cover and simmer 1 hour or until steak is tender. (Or cover and bake at 350 degrees.) Serve over beds of fluffy rice. Makes 6 servings.

Farm Style Bear

INGREDIENTS

Marinate bear stew meat in buttermilk and a tenderizer overnight. Wash thoroughly.
1 lb. Bear Stew Meat
2 tbsp. bacon fat
1/2 bag baby Carrots
2 diced Onions
3 diced Celery Stalks
1/2 tbsp. Garlic Powder
Salt and pepper
1 cup sherry wine

Dice bear meat into fork size portions. Brown quickly in bacon fat. Put bear meat, vegetables, seasonings and enough water to cover meat in a pot. Cover pot tightly and simmer until tender over low heat. Blend vegetables to thicken gravy and simmer, add water if necessary to thicken as needed.

Correct seasonings and serve.

Bear Meat Balls

INGREDIENTS

2 lbs. ground bear meat
1 tsp. garlic 1/2 cup chopped onion
1/2 cup oatmeal
1 tsp. salt
One half tsp. pepper

Mix. Form into balls. Brown in oil in frying pan. Deglaze pan, Add 2 tbsp. flour and water to make gravy, cover and simmer for 1 hour.

Bear Roast #1

INGREDIENTS

1 1/4 tsp. paprika
1 tsp. salt
1/4 tsp. pepper
1/2 tsp. seasoned salt
1 1/2 tbsp. instant minced onion
1 cup beef bouillon

Rub all sides of bear meat with the first four ingredients. Place seasoned meat in crock pot, sprinkle with onion and pour bouillon over all. Cook on high setting for 1 1/2 to 2 hours per pound until 180 degrees F. (check internal temp. of thickest part of roast with meat thermometer). Vegetables such as carrots, potatoes, and celery may be added and cooked the same amount of time as the meat. For gravy: remove meat from pot; stir flour in small amount of water and add to meat juices. Serves 6.

Bear Roast #2

INGREDIENTS

3-4 lbs. young bear roast
1/4 cup cooking oil
1 garlic clove
1 minced onion
1/3 cup red wine
4 carrots
3 stalks celery, diced
1 1/3 cup water
2 tbsp. sugar
1/2 tsp. chili powder
2 tbsp. dry mustard
1/4 tsp. pepper
1/2 cup tomato paste
2 tsp. salt

Place roast in a skillet and add cooking oil. Braise roast on all sides using high heat. Add remaining ingredients and simmer for 30 minutes. Place roast and sauce in an open pan and cook for 3-4 hours at 350 degrees.

Baste often. At the end, remove the vegetables and blend to thicken sauce.

Roast should be served well done. Serves 6-8.

BEAVER RECIPES

Important Read This First:

Chef Gahagan says, always marinate meat in Buttermilk and Meat Tenderizer for about three hours. Then wash off the buttermilk and remarinate in wine and herbs if desired.

Sauteed Beaver

1 small Beaver (20 lbs.), cleaned and skinned, cut into serving pieces, strips or cubes
6 slices bacon
1 tsp. seasoning salt

Remove fat from Beaver and soak overnight in cold water. Drain. Cook in small amount of water until tender, then fry with bacon and seasoning salt.

Variation: substitute hickory-smoked seasoning salt for plain seasoning salt.

Baked Beaver

1 Beaver (8-10 lbs.)
1 bay leaf
2 med. onions
1-2 garlic cloves
Celery leaves—optional
4 carrots diced
1 tbsp.sugar
2 tsp. Thyme
Flour
Salt and pepper

Remove all fat from Beaver. Cut up as you do rabbit. Soak overnight in salt water. Marinate in buttermilk. Parboil until about half-cooked in water with the bay leaf, onions, garlic, celery and seasonings. Drain, roll in flour and brown in bacon fat, season with salt and pepper. Bake in covered pan in a moderate oven until tender. Gravy may be made from the drippings. Plan the same number of servings as from a similar weight of pork (8 oz. per serving). Beaver is very rich.

Roased and Barbecued Beaver

1 small to medium Beaver or raccoon cut into serving size pieces
1/2 tsp. salt
1 teaspoon instant minced onion
3 tbsp. brown sugar
1/2 cup barbecue sauce of Italian Salad Dressing
1 1/2 teaspoon garlic
1 (7 oz.) bottle of beer or pickle juice

Place pieces of Beaver or raccoon in a foil-lined roasting pan. Preheat oven to 350 degrees F. and roast, covered for a half hour. Meanwhile, mix other ingredients in a small bowl for barbecue sauce. After meat has roasted a half hour, uncover and pour barbecue sauce over the pieces. Then roast, uncovered, for another half hour to an hour—until tender. Baste several times during cooking, using your barbecue sauce.

Beaver Tail

Hold over open flame until rough skin blisters. Remove from heat. When cool, peel off skin. Roast over coals or simmer until tender while basting with barbecue sauce

Beaver in Sour Cream

2-3 lbs. 1 inch cubes Beaver
Bacon fat
1/2 cups flour
1 1/2 tsp. sugar
1 tsp. salt
1 tsp.pepper
2 medium onions
1/2 tsp.tyme
1/2 tsp.tarragon
1/2 lb. carrots
3 celery stalks
6 medium potatoes
2 garlic cloves

Combine flour, salt and pepper in a closable bag or 2 quart closable plastic container and shake until mixed. Add Beaver and shake until well coated.

Dice onions. Melt enough bacon fat in the bottom of a fry pan to saute onions and Beaver. Saute onions and floured Beaver in bacon fat, adding more fat as needed. Place sauted cubes and onions in a 4 quart pot with enough water to cover. Add water to fry pan to deglaze the pan. Add this pan gravy to your stew. Slice carrots and dice celery. Add carrots and celery to your stew and simmer until Beaver is somewhat tender (about 30 minutes). Taste broth and add salt or pepper to taste. Cook potatoes separately until soft. Simmer until potatoes are done.

Beaver Stew

2-4 lbs. cut Beaver
1/2 cup flour
1 tsp. salt
1/4 tsp. paprika
1/2 tsp. salt
1/2 cup water
1 cup sour cream
Oil to cover
1 onion

Clean Beaver and soak overnight in salted water (1 tbsp. salt to 1 quart water). Drain, cut up, and roll in 1/2 cup flour seasoned with 1 tsp. salt and 1/4 tsp. paprika. Fry in fat until browned. Then cover the Beaver with sliced onion. Sprinkle the onion slices with 1/2 tsp. salt. Add 1/2 cup water. Cover the skillet tightly. Simmer for 1 hour. Add 1 cup sour cream the last 15 minutes of cooking time. Serves 2-4 depending on the size of the animal.

Deep Fried Beaver

2-4 lbs. cut Beaver
1/2 cup flour
1 tsp. salt
1/4 tsp. paprika
1/2 tsp. salt
1/2 cup water
1 cup sour cream
Oil to cover
1 onion

Clean Beaver and soak overnight in salted water (1 tbsp. salt to 1 quart water). Drain, cut up, and roll in 1/2 cup flour seasoned with 1 tsp. salt and 1/4 tsp. paprika. Fry in fat until browned. Then cover the Beaver with sliced onion. Sprinkle the onion slices with 1/2 tsp. salt. Add 1/2 cup water. Cover the skillet tightly. Simmer for 1 hour. Add 1 cup sour cream the last 15 minutes of cooking time. Serves 2-4 depending on the size of the animal.

Country Style Beaver

2-4 lbs. cut Beaver
1/2 cup flour
1 tsp. salt
1/4 tsp. paprika
1/2 tsp. salt
1/2 cup water
1 cup sour cream
Oil to cover
1 onion

Clean Beaver and soak overnight in salted water (1 tbsp. salt to 1 quart water). Drain, cut up, and roll in 1/2 cup flour seasoned with 1 tsp. salt and 1/4 tsp. paprika. Fry in fat until browned. Then cover the Beaver with sliced onion. Sprinkle the onion slices with 1/2 tsp. salt. Add 1/2 cup water. Cover the skillet tightly. Simmer for 1 hour. Add 1 cup sour cream the last 15 minutes of cooking time. Serves 2-4 depending on the size of the animal.

Pot Roasted Beaver

One Beaver Quartered
4 ounces of Bacon Fat
4 carrots scraped
1 large onion
2 gasrlic cloves
1 tbsp.brown sugar
3 CelerynStalks
1 tsp.Accent (MSG) 1 tpsp oregano
1/4 tsp. cinnamon
3 tbsp.tomato paste
Salt and pepper

Brown Beaver in bacon fat in large pot. When done add vegetables and seasonings, cover with water and simmer for one and a half hours. Remove veggetables and blend with sufficient water. Add pureed vegeytables back to pot. Correct seasonings and serve.

Roast Beaver

One small or medium size Beaver, cleaned and skinned
Baking soda
Sliced onions
Bacon

Remove all surface fat. Marinate in buttermilk overnight. Rinse and then boil 10 minutes and drain. Cover Beaver with bacon and onions and roast until tender. This will taste like roast goose and will fool anybody.

BOAR RECIPES

Our Favorite Boar Recipe

Important Read This First:

Chef Gahagan says always marinate Wild Boar in Buttermilk and Meat Tenderizer for about three hours. Then wash off the buttermilk and remarinate in wine and herbs if desired.

Ingredients
8 pieces of thin sliced Boar loin or tenderloin
2 tbsp. Bacon Fat
1/2 lemon cut in two pieces
1/2 tsp. Garlic powder
1/2 tsp. MSG (MSG)
4 oz. Sherry or White Wine

Directions

Mix seasonings and Parmesan.
Deglaze the pan with Sherry and
pour over Boar slices
Squeeze lemon over Boar and serve.
1 tsp. Parmesan Cheese per serving
Sprinkle seasonings onto boar slices.
Very lightly warm Boar in bacon fat until tender

Easy Wild Boar in Cheese Pasta

Important Read This First:

Chef Gahagan says always marinate Wild Boar in Buttermilk and Meat Tenderizer for about three hours. Then wash off the buttermilk and remarinate in wine and herbs if desired.

Ingredients

2 cups any small Pasts (rotini, shells, Penne, etc.
3 cups of Cooked bite size pieces of Wild Boar
1 can corn
1 jar Pasta Sauce
1 tsp. MSG
1 tbsp. oil
1 cup Shredded Cheese (your choice)
1 tbsp. oil

Directions:

Cook Pasta with oil to prevent sticking according to pkg. Directions

Mix all ingredients together and top with shredded Cheese while still hot.

Bake at 350 F until cheese is melted.

Wild Boar Kabobs Teryaki

Important Read This First:

Chef Gahagan says always marinate Wild Boar in Buttermilk and Meat Tenderizer for about three hours. Then wash off the buttermilk and remarinate in wine and herbs if desired.

Ingredients

1 1/2 lbs. of boneless Wild Boar loin, in 1 inch cubes
2 tbsp. cornstarch
1 3/4 cups Beef Stock
2 tbsp. Teriyaki sauce
1/2 tsp. garlic powder
12 medium mushrooms
1 large onion, cut in 12 wedges
4 cups cooked white rice

Directions

Stir the cornstarch, stock, Teriyaki sauce and garlic powder in a 2-quart saucepan until the mixture is smooth. Cook and stir over medium heat until the mixture boils and thickens. Remove the saucepan from the heat.

Thread alternately the Wild Boar, mushrooms and onion on 4 skewers.

Lightly oil the grill rack and heat the grill to medium.

Grill the kabobs until the Wild Boar is golden brown. Turn it often and brush with the stock mixture. Thread 1 tomato on each skewer.

Heat the remaining stock mixture to a boil over medium-high heat. Serve the stock mixture with the kabobs and rice. Serves 4.

Easy Wild Boar in Peach Sauce

Important Read This First:

Chef Gahagan says always marinate Wild Boar in Buttermilk and Meat Tenderizer for about three hours. Then wash off the buttermilk and remarinate in wine and herbs if desired.

Ingredients

4 Wild Boar Chops
4 tbsp. butter
1/2 lb. Mozzarella Cheese

Directions:

Broil Wild Boar Chops until tender

Open Broiler. Put one slice of Mozzarella Cheese on each Chop and top with 1 tbsp. parmesan.

Reheat gently for 1 minute in the broiler.

Wild Boar in Apricot Sauce

Important Read This First:

Chef Gahagan says always marinate Wild Boar in Buttermilk and Meat Tenderizer for about three hours. Then wash off the buttermilk and remarinate in wine and herbs if desired.

Ingredients

2 cups of Wild Boar in bite size pieces
1/4 cup melted Butter
1 1/4 olive oil
Paprika for color
2 tsp. Sage
1 can Apricots
1 cup light cream
1/2 tsp. MSG

Directions

First drain Apricots and blend with Cream, Dill and MSG on high.

Then, pour into a pot and slowly simmer until thickened.

The Wild Boar

Sprinkle Wild Boar pieces with paprika, place them in a skillet with melted butter and oil mix.

Warm the Wild Boar in oil. Cover with top if necessary. Add butter at end.

Place them in a Casserole dish and top with Apricot Cream Sauce. Preheat until warm and serve.

East Wild Boar Acapulco

Important Read This First:

Chef Gahagan says always marinate Wild Boar in Buttermilk and Meat Tenderizer for about three hours. Then wash off the buttermilk and remarinate in wine and herbs if desired.

Ingredients

3 cups of boar loin
1 jar Salsa your choice of hot
1 can Cheddar Cheese soup
1/2 can milk
4 tbsp. Bacon fat
1 can Artichoke Hearts
1 pkg. Shredded. Monterey Jack Cheese

Directions:

Mix and heat Soup, milk and Salsa

Ver gently Sauté Wild Boar pieces until tender in a large pot

Add soup and Salsa mix.

Top with Monterey Jack Cheese and decorate with Artichoke Hearts. Serve with rice. Feed 6.

Wild Boar in Artichoke Honey Sauce

Important Read This First:

Chef Gahagan says always marinate Wild Boar in Buttermilk and Meat Tenderizer for about three hours. Then wash off the buttermilk and remarinate in wine and herbs if desired.

Ingredients

2 cups of sliced Wild Boar Loin cut into bite size pieces
1 1/2 cups heavy cream
1 can of the small artichoke hearts (Large size are too tough)
1 lb. Bacon, microwaved well done
Paprika for color
2 tsp. Garlic Powder
2 tbsp. Dijon Mustard
4 ounces of honey extra milk

Directions

Blend Artichokes, cream, honey, mustard and Garlic Powder on high.

Place Wild Boar in Casserole and cover with sauce.

Crumble well done bacon on top of sauce

Then, Do not boil but slowly simmer until Wild Boar is tender. Add milk as needed to maintain moisture

Boar with Crumpled Bacon

Important Read This First:

Chef Gahagan says always marinate Wild Boar in Buttermilk and Meat Tenderizer for about three hours. Then wash off the buttermilk and remarinate in wine and herbs if desired.

Ingredients

6 Wild Boar Chops
3 tbsp. olive oil
1 lb. well done crumpled Bacon
1 pkg. white sauce
2 tbsp. Parmesan cheese
Directions

Sauté Wild Boar Chops 4 minutes on each side in bacon fat. When the Wild Boar is done, place it on your serving platter and cover with the sauce.

Sauce, the Easy Way

Buy a pkg. of prepared white sauce (Bechamel). Prepare it according to package Directions. If the recipe instructs you to use butter, use bacon fat instead for more flavor.

Add the well done crumpled bacon and the Parmesan cheese to sauce and you are done.

Our Chef Says: Most gourmet Recipes are too complicated because most chefs think it makes them look more knowledgeable. Forget it. Always search for the "Easy" version of a recipe on any Search Engine `

Wild Boar in Peach Sauce

Important Read This First:

Chef Gahagan says always marinate Wild Boar in Buttermilk and Meat Tenderizer for about three hours. Then wash off the buttermilk and remarinate in wine and herbs if desired.

Ingredients

2 cups Wild Boar pieces
2 cans sliced Peaches, or better, Fresh Peaches
1 cup light cream
1/2 tsp. MSG
2 tsp. Oregano
2 tsp. Sage
1 tsp. Garlic powder
4 tbsp. sugar
Salt and Pepper to taste
1 tsp. MSG

Directions

Saute pieces of Wild Boar until warm.

Mix Oregano OR Sage powder with Garlic powder and cream

Drain Cans of sliced peaches and blend peaches with light cream, MSG and sugar

Mix Wild Boar and peach sauce in a Casserole dish. Adjust seasonings and serve.

Easy Zucchini Wild Boar

Important Read This First:

Chef Gahagan says always marinate Wild Boar in Buttermilk and Meat Tenderizer for about three hours. Then wash off the buttermilk and remarinate in wine and herbs if desired.

Ingredients

3 cups Wild Boar scissored to bite size
2 cans Zucchini in tomato sauce
1 large onion
1 tsp. Garlic Powder
1/2 cup Shredded Cheddar or Parmesan cheese
1 tbsp. sugar

Directions:

Preheat oven to 350 F.

Oil a casserole with bacon fat. Put in Wild Boar. Top with Zucchini sauce.

Add Shredded Cheese. Bake until done.

Barbecued Wild Boar Chops

Important Read This First:

Chef Gahagan says always marinate Wild Boar in Buttermilk and Meat Tenderizer for about three hours. Then wash off the buttermilk and remarinate in wine and herbs if desired.

Ingredients

1 lb. Wild Boar Loin or 4 chops 3/4 inch thick
2 tbsp. Bacon Fat
1 large chopped onion
1 can Cheddar Cheese soup
1/2 cup Hickory smoked Barbecue Sauce
1/2 cup milk
1 tsp. chili powder
1 tsp. MSG

Directions

Use a 2-quart saucepan over medium heat to saute the onion for 5 minutes or until it is golden. Stir the soup, milk, chili powder, MSG and barbecue sauce. Reduce the heat to low. Cook and stir for 3 minutes or until the mixture is hot and bubbling. Remove the saucepan from the heat and keep warm.

Lightly oil the grill rack and heat the grill to medium. Grill the Boar for 2 1/2 minutes a side turning the Boar over once during grilling. Spoon the sauce over the boar. Serves 4.

Wild Boar a la King

Important Read This First:

Chef Gahagan says always marinate Wild Boar in Buttermilk and Meat Tenderizer for about three hours. Then wash off the buttermilk and remarinate in wine and herbs if desired.

Ingredients

2 cups of cooked Wild Boar cut into bit size pieces
2 pkgs. white sauce* butter
1 tsp. garlic powder
1 tsp. onion powder
1 tsp. sugar
1 tsp. Sage
2 tsp. paprika

Directions

Make sauce According to package Directions mixing a herbs.

Put Wild Boar in a serving dish

Top with Paprika and serve

Wild Boar in Red Wine

Important Read This First:

Chef Gahagan says always marinate Wild Boar in Buttermilk and Meat Tenderizer for about three hours. Then wash off the buttermilk and remarinate in wine and herbs if desired.

Ingredients

4 Wild Boar leg steaks or chops
1 tomato
2 cups Port wine
1/2 tsp. Sage
1/2 tsp. Thyme
1/2 tsp. MSG salt and pepper to taste

Directions

Put all ingredients in a pot and simmer until Wild Boar is very tender and falls off the bone. Add water as necessary.

Serve with baby carrots

Wild Boar Avila

Important Read This First:

Chef Gahagan says always marinate Wild Boar in Buttermilk and Meat Tenderizer for about three hours. Then wash off the buttermilk and remarinate in wine and herbs if desired.

Ingredients

3 cups bite size Wild Boar pieces
2 jars salsa (your choice of hot)
1 can Cheddar Cheese Soup
1 cup Port wine
4 tbsp. Olive oil

Directions

Preheat oven to 300F

Put butter and Wild Boar in an oven proof pot and saute until tender Mix Soup, Wine and Salsa; add to the pot and bake at 300 F until tender.

Add liquid as necessary

Wild Boar Carbonara

Important Read This First:

Chef Gahagan says always marinate Wild Boar in Buttermilk and Meat Tenderizer for about three hours. Then wash off the buttermilk and remarinate in wine and herbs if desired.

Ingredients

3 cups of Wild Boar Leftovers
1 pkg. Egg Noodles
8 slices bacon
1 tsp. Garlic powder
2 tsp. pepper
2 pkg. white sauce mix
1/2 cup Parmesan cheese
1 tsp. Sugar
1 cup milk
I can black olives

Directions

Scissor Leftovers into bite size pieces.

Cook 4 cups of Noodles according to package directions.

Cook bacon until crisp. Drain and save.

Prepare white sauce mix. Add Parmesan cheese, Bacon, Garlic powder and sugar.

Put cooked noodles on the bottom of a baking pan greased with Bacon Fat. Sprinkle Wild Boar on top of noodles,.

Cover Boar with sauce and decorate with Black Olives. Heat and serve.

Easy Boar Casserole

Important Read This First:

Chef Gahagan says always marinate Wild Boar in Buttermilk and Meat Tenderizer for about three hours. Then wash off the buttermilk and remarinate in wine and herbs if desired.
This is an adaptation of the famous French dish, Sole With Crumpled Bacon

Ingredients

3 cups Wild Boar leftovers
1 Kielb.asa scissored in bite size pieces
1 cup meat stock
1 pkg. White sauce or Bechamel
3 tbsp. Bacon fat
1/2 lb. well done crumpled Bacon
1/2 pkg. cooked baby carrots

Directions

Put Wild Boar, meat stock and Kielb.asa in a Casserole dish with 2 tbsp. Bacon fat and bake for 1/2 hour.

Sauce, the Easy Way

Prepare pkgd. sauce according to Directions. Stir in 3 extra ounces of milk and an extra tbsp. each of bacon fat and flour to add flavor.

Add the carrots and crumpled bacon and the sauce is done.

Cover the Wild Boar with the sauce and serve when ready.

Wild Boar and Cottage Cheese Casserole

Our Chef Says: This is a very nutritious, inexpensive dish

Important Read This First:

Chef Gahagan says always marinate Wild Boar in Buttermilk and Meat Tenderizer for about three hours. Then wash off the buttermilk and remarinate in wine and herbs if desired.

Ingredients

3 cups Pulled or cooked Loin of Wild Boar in bite size pieces.
2 cups any small Pasts (rotini, shells, Penne, etc.
1 cup cottage Cheese
1 can corn
1 cup milk
1 tsp. MSG
1 tbsp. Oil or Bacon Fat
1 cup Shredded Cheese (your choice)

Directions:

Drain Can of Corn

Cook Pasta with oil to prevent sticking according to pkg. Directions

Mix all ingredients. Top with Shredded cheese and Bake at 300 F until cheese is melted.

Wild Boar Curry

Important Read This First:

Chef Gahagan says always marinate Wild Boar in Buttermilk and Meat Tenderizer for about three hours. Then wash off the buttermilk and remarinate in wine and herbs if desired.

Ingredients

3 cups of cooked Wild Boar cut into bite size pieces
2 pkgs. of Curry sauce*
2 sticks of butter
1/2 tsp. garlic powder
1 tsp. onion powder
1 tsp. sugar
1 small pkg. Peanuts
2-3 tsp. Curry powder (if needed)
1-1/2 cup Raisins and/or scissored prunes

Directions

Make a Curry sauce according to pkg. Directions or follow the recipe below. If your store does not have a curry sauce mix, buy a white sauce mix and add Curry powder
Mix in raisins, peanuts and scissored prunes

Put Wild Boar in a serving dish, add sauce and decorate with paprika and/or pieces of canned apricots, mushrooms or peaches as you desire.

Preheat and serve.

*Recipe for Curry sauce from scratch.

Melt 5 tbsp. butter in a double boiler. Add 6 tbsp. Flour. Heat and stir together into a roux.

Slowly add 2 cups of milk stirring continually. Add salt and pepper to taste and 1/2 tsp. Garlic and Onion powder, raisins and prunes and 2-3

Easy Boar Curry Casserole

Important Read This First:

Chef Gahagan says always marinate Wild Boar in Buttermilk and Meat Tenderizer for about three hours. Then wash off the buttermilk and remarinate in wine and herbs if desired.

Ingredients

2 cups cooked rice
1 can red beans
2 cups Wild Boar pieces, preferably leftovers
2 tbsp. Bacon Fat
1 can Chicken Soup
10 baby carrots
2 tbsp. curry powder
1 tsp. Sugar
1/2 cup milk
1 tsp. MSG

Directions

If necessary, Saute Wild Boar and cook Carrots.

Mix all together in a big pot. Add more or use less curry powder to taste.

Serve with chutney

Wild Boar Florentinene

Important Read This First:

Chef Gahagan says always marinate Wild Boar in Buttermilk and Meat Tenderizer for about three hours. Then wash off the buttermilk and remarinate in wine and herbs if desired.

Ingredients

1 lb. Wild Boar Fillet, sliced thin
1 cup milk
1 tsp. dill
3 cups cooked Noodles
1/4 tsp. Garlic powder
Salt and Pepper to taste
1 pkg. Frozen Creamed spinach

Directions

Cook Noodles according to Directions.

Put Wild Boar Fillets, milk, garlic powder, Dill, salt and pepper into a skillet and cook until the Wild Boar Fillets are done to your liking.

Cook frozen creamed spinach according to package Directions.

Place Noodles on a serving dish. Top with Wild Boar. Cut a corner off the plastic frozen spinach pkg. and squeeze Contents onto the Boar and serve.

Serves 4

Wild Boar with Grapes

This is an adaptation of the famous French dish, Sole With Grapes.

The dish originated in the farm country of Normandy near where the Americans landed in WWII. It is sometimes made with both apples and grapes as Normandy is famous for its apples and Apple Brandy (Calvados).

Like most country Recipes, it is very simple and delicious if made well.

Important Read This First:

Chef Gahagan says always marinate Wild Boar in Buttermilk and Meat Tenderizer for about three hours. Then wash off the buttermilk and remarinate in wine and herbs if desired.

Ingredients

4 Wild Boar Chops or 1 lb. Of diced Wild Boar
3 tbsp. olive oil
2 pkgs. of white sauce
1 bunch Seedless Grapes
1 cup Sherry or Port and water to cover meat
1 tsp. sugar

Directions

Sauce, the Easy Way

Buy 2 pkg. of prepared white sauce. Fix it according to Directions. Stir in an extra egg yolk to make it richer. Add the grapes to the sauce, heat and you are done with the sauce.

Simmer Wild Boar in wine, sherry and water until very tender. When the Wild Boar is done, place it on your serving platter and cover it with the sauce and top with grapes

Honey Mustard Boar

Important Read This First:

Chef Gahagan says always marinate Wild Boar in Buttermilk and Meat Tenderizer for about three hours. Then wash off the buttermilk and remarinate in wine and herbs if desired.

Ingredients

2 lbs. Wild Boar Chops
1/2 cup of Honey Mustard
1/4 cup butter
1/4 cup Hickory smoked Barbecue Sauce
1/2 tsp. MSG (MSG)
Bread Crumbs
2 tbsp. Olive oil
1 tbsp. Extra honey

Directions

Mix MSG, honey mustard, honey and butter together

Coat or cover boar with all the Honey Mustard mix

Dip in Breadcrumbs

Bake until tender.

Note: seal Casserole top with aluminum foil. Add milk if necessary.

Wild Boar Chops in Irish Cream Sauce

Important Read This First:

Chef Gahagan says always marinate Wild Boar in Buttermilk and Meat Tenderizer for about three hours. Then wash off the buttermilk and remarinate in wine and herbs if desired.

Ingredients

4 Wild Boar Chops
Salt and pepper
1/3 cup melted butter
1/2 cup Irish Cream Whiskey
Can Sliced Peaches (or fresh peaches)

Directions

Cook bacon well done in microwave

Sprinkle pepper on Wild Boar and sauté gently until tender.

Deglaze pan and pour off fat. Add a slice or two of peaches on top of the chops. Cover with Irish Cream for a sauce.

Grilled Boar Italiano

Important Read This First:

Chef Gahagan says always marinate Wild Boar in Buttermilk and Meat Tenderizer for about three hours. Then wash off the buttermilk and remarinate in wine and herbs if desired.

Ingredients

4 Wild Boar Chops
1 Bottle Italian Salad Dressing
4 ounces your Marmalade, Peach or Apricot Jam

Directions:

Marinate first in buttermilk. Then wash off buttermilk and remarinate

Wild Boar in Salad Dressing for at least 1 hour

Sauté, Broil or grill chops until tender.

Heat jam and cover chops with jam and serve

Easy Wild Boar Loaf

Important Read This First:

Chef Gahagan says always marinate Wild Boar in Buttermilk and Meat Tenderizer for about three hours. Then wash off the buttermilk and remarinate in wine and herbs if desired.

Ingredients

1 1/2 lbs. Ground Wild Boar
1 chopped large Onion
1 tbsp. Hickory Smoked Barbecue Sauce
1 tsp. sage
1 tsp. Garlic Powder
1/2 cup Port Wine
6 slices of bacon
1 tbsp. flour

Directions

Preheat oven and mix all ingredients (except bacon) together

Put in a baking pan and bake for 3/4 to 1 hour

Top with bacon slices

Easy Boar Cassoulet (French Boar with Beans)

Important Read This First:

Chef Gahagan says always marinate Wild Boar in Buttermilk and Meat Tenderizer for about three hours. Then wash off the buttermilk and remarinate in wine and herbs if desired.

Ingredients

2 cups of Boar Breasts cut into bite size pieces
2 tbsp. melted Butter
Paprika for color

Chef's Note: This is an adaptation of the famous French dish, Cassoulet de Strasbourg. Actually, there are three different Cassoulet.
This one, the Classic Cassoulet de Perigord, which is made with goose, the Cassoulet d'Auvergne which is made with lamb

Ingredients

3 cups diced Boar
1 bag or four cans of Great Northern Beans
1 Bratwurst Sliced
1 Knockwurst Sliced
1/2 Kielb.asa Sliced
1 can Italian Stewed Tomatoes blended on high
1 pkg. Onion Soup Mix
2 Onions diced
1 pkg. Onion dip Mix
10 baby carrots
3 tbsp. Bacon fat
1/2 tsp. MSG

Directions

If you plan to cook a bag of beans, follow package directions. Then add the remaining ingredients.
Put all ingredients in a pot and simmer at a low heat until the Boar is tender
Stir frequently and add water as needed because the beans tend to stick to the bottom of the pot Salt and pepper to taste

Delicious Hawaiian Boar

Important Read This First:

Chef Gahagan says always marinate Wild Boar in Buttermilk and Meat Tenderizer for about three hours. Then wash off the buttermilk and remarinate in wine and herbs if desired.

3 cups pulled Boar or leftovers
1 can Pineapple Chunks
2 cups Heavy cream
1 tsp. MSG
Salt and Pepper to taste

Directions

First prepare the Pineapple Sauce.
Drain Pineapple Juice. Reserve chunks. Puree juice with cream and MSG.
Then, put it in a pot and slowly simmer until thickened.

The Boar

Sprinkle Boar with salt and pepper and Saute pieces of Boar until tender.

Place Boar pieces in a Casserole dish, top with Pineapple Chunks and cover with Cream Sauce. Sprinkle Paprika.

Heat until warm and serve.

Wild Boar in a Creamy Pecan Sauce

Important Read This First:

Chef Gahagan says always marinate Wild Boar in Buttermilk and Meat Tenderizer for about three hours. Then wash off the buttermilk and remarinate in wine and herbs if desired.

Ingredients

4 Boar Chops
1 pkg. White (Bechamel) Sauce
4 tbsp. butter
3 1/2 ounces Pecan bits
1/2 cup honey
3 tbsp. water
Salt and pepper to taste

Directions

Chop Pecan bits in food processor or blender and Pecans in 1 tbsp. butter

Remove Pecans, add the rest of the butter and sauté Boar Chops until done, turning so both sides are coated with butter.

Add the honey back into the pan, add water and stir together.

Put the Boar on a serving plate. Then deglaze the pan and pour the Pecan, Honey/Butter sauce over the Boar Chops.

Serve Boar Chops hot

Easy Crusted Country Boar

Important Read This First:

Chef Gahagan says always marinate Wild Boar in Buttermilk and Meat Tenderizer for about three hours. Then wash off the buttermilk and remarinate in wine and herbs if desired.

Ingredients

2 cups of Boar diced small
1 forked egg
3 tbsp. Bisquick
1 cup milk
1 tsp. Sage powder
1 cup Corn Flakes
6 tbsp. Butter
Salt and Pepper to taste

Directions:

Make a white sauce by mixing the Bisquick with three tbsp. Bacon fat and then slowly adding milk

Crush Corn flakes and mix with Salt, Pepper, eggs and Sage.

Dip Boar in forked eggs

Dip Boar in Bisquick mix

Dip Boar in Corn Flake mix

Place on a baking sheet. Turn once and bake until golden brown

Easy Danish Boar

Important Read This First:

Chef Gahagan says always marinate Wild Boar in Buttermilk and Meat Tenderizer for about three hours. Then wash off the buttermilk and remarinate in wine and herbs if desired.

Ingredients

2 cups diced Boar
4 tbsp. butter
1 cup White Sauce with Mushrooms
1 tsp. Dark Rum
4 ounces of Danish Blue Cheese

Directions:

Make White Sauce according to Pkg. Directions.

Mix in mushrooms and Danish Blue Cheese

Scissor Boar into bite size pieces.

Cook Boar and butter in a pot, Stirring occasionally so it does not stick together.

When tender, Add White (Bechamel) Sauce with Danish Blue Cheese and rum when Boar is almost done.

Easy Elegant Boar Chops

Important Read This First:

Chef Gahagan says always marinate Wild Boar in Buttermilk and Meat Tenderizer for about three hours. Then wash off the buttermilk and remarinate in wine and herbs if desired.

Ingredients

6 Boar Chops
1 can Mushroom Soup
4-5 ounces Sherry Wine
1/2 tsp. Garlic or Onion Powder
1/2 cup Stilton Cheese
1 can Black Olives

Directions

Scissor fat off Boar Chops and put them in a casserole dish

Mix all other ingredients together, heat and pour over Boar Chops

Bake until Chops reach 140 F. Decorate with Black Olives and serve.

Easy Ginger Boar

Important Read This First:

Chef Gahagan says always marinate Wild Boar in Buttermilk and Meat Tenderizer for about three hours. Then wash off the buttermilk and remarinate in wine and herbs if desired.

Ingredients

2 cups bite size leftover Boar bits
2 tsp. Soy Sauce
1 tbsp. Ginger
1 tsp. Cornstarch
1 cup water
1 tbsp. Tomato paste
1 tsp. MSG

Directions

Mix all ingredients together and simmer until done

Check to add fluid when necessary.

Easy Grilled Garlic Boar Chops

Important Read This First:

Chef Gahagan says always marinate Wild Boar in Buttermilk and Meat Tenderizer for about three hours. Then wash off the buttermilk and remarinate in wine and herbs if desired.

Ingredients

4 1/4 lb. Boar Chops
1 tbsp. vegetable oil
2 tsp. Garlic powder
1 can Mushroom Soup
1 tsp. Ground Sage
1 cup Sherry wine
1 tsp. MSG
4 cups hot cooked couscous or long-grain white rice

Directions:

Grill or sauté the chops to 140 F. Remove the chops and set aside.

Stir the soup, garlic, MSG and milk into the skillet. Heat to a boil. Return the chops to the skillet. Serve with couscous or rice. Serves 4.

Italian Boar Stew

Important Read This First:

Chef Gahagan says always marinate Wild Boar in Buttermilk and Meat Tenderizer for about three hours. Then wash off the buttermilk and remarinate in wine and herbs if desired.

Ingredients

2 lbs. Boar tenderloin
1 chopped medium onion
1 lb. Bacon cooked crisp
2 tsp. garlic powder
1 jar your favorite pasts sauce
1/2 cup Parmesan cheese
12 baby carrots
2 tsp. oregano
2 tsp. Garlic powder
2 cups cooked spaghetti

Directions

Mix vegetables, seasonings, spaghetti sauce, and Parmesan cheese in a pot. Simmer till done adding water if necessary.

Add Boar and Spaghetti.

Easy Mandarin Boar

Important Read This First:

Chef Gahagan says always marinate Wild Boar in Buttermilk and Meat Tenderizer for about three hours. Then wash off the buttermilk and remarinate in wine and herbs if desired.

Ingredients

8 thin or 4 thick slices of Boar fillet
2 tbsp. butter
1 can drained Mandarin Oranges
4 ounces Cointreau or Orange liquor

Directions:

Slice Boar fillet crosswise

Butter a baking pan and put Boar slices on it, overlapping with orange slices in between

Bake until warm. Add Cointreau and serve

Elegant, Delicious Mayo Boar

Important Read This First:

Chef Gahagan says always marinate Wild Boar in Buttermilk and Meat Tenderizer for about three hours. Then wash off the buttermilk and remarinate in wine and herbs if desired.

Ingredients

1 pound Thin Sliced Boar
1/2 cup Italian bread crumbs
3 tbsp. Butter
2-3 tbsp. mayonnaise
1 tsp. Oregano
1 tsp. Garlic powder
Pinch of salt and pepper

Directions

Put the Boar Slices in a buttered pan. Spoon a thin layer of mayonnaise on top.

Then sprinkle both sides with the bread crumbs, oregano, salt, pepper and garlic powder

Cover the pan and cook until tender.

Easy French Boar and Beans

Important Read This First:

Chef Gahagan says always marinate Wild Boar in Buttermilk and Meat Tenderizer for about three hours. Then wash off the buttermilk and remarinate in wine and herbs if desired.

Ingredients

3 cups diced Boar
1 bag or four cans of Great Northern Beans
1 Kielb.asa Sliced
1 can Italian Stewed Tomatoes blended on high
1 pkg. Onion Soup Mix
2 Onions diced
1 pkg. Onion dip Mix
10 baby carrots
3 tbsp. Bacon fat
1/2 tsp. MSG
1 cup water

Directions

If you plan to cook a bag of beans, follow package directions. Then add the remaining ingredients.

Put all ingredients in a pot and simmer at a low heat for 1 hour or until the Boar is tender

Stir frequently and add water as needed because the beans tend to stick to the bottom of the pot

Easy German Boar Loaf #2

Important Read This First:

Chef Gahagan says always marinate Wild Boar in Buttermilk and Meat Tenderizer for about three hours. Then wash off the buttermilk and remarinate in wine and herbs if desired.

Ingredients:
1 lb. Ground Boar
1 tbsp. Sugar
1 onion finely diced
1 diced Knockwurst
1 diced Bratwurst
Salt and pepper to taste
3/4 cup oatmeal to act as a binder
1/4 cup bacon fat, oil or butter
1 cup Spaghetti Sauce

Directions:

Mix all ingredients except the spaghetti sauce and place in an oiled loaf pan.

Bake at 350 F for 1 hour

Heat Spaghetti Sauce and serve with the Meatloaf.

Easy Ginger Boar

Important Read This First:

Chef Gahagan says always marinate Wild Boar in Buttermilk and Meat Tenderizer for about three hours. Then wash off the buttermilk and remarinate in wine and herbs if desired.

Ingredients

1 lb. Boar cut in strips and marinated
2 tbsp. cornstarch
1 3/4 cans of Chicken broth
2 tbsp. soy sauce
3 tbsp. Olive Oil
3 cups frozen Peas
2 cups frozen Lima beans
3/4 tsp. garlic powder
2 tsp. ground ginger

Half freeze and cut Boar into bite size strips

Mix cornstarch, broth and soy.

Sauté Boar until browned. Remove and keep warm

Sauté vegetables, garlic powder and ginger until vegetables are tender-crisp.

Add cornstarch mixture until mixture boils and thickens. Add Boar to skillet and heat through.

Easy Ginger Zucchini Boar

Important Read This First:

Chef Gahagan says always marinate Wild Boar in Buttermilk and Meat Tenderizer for about three hours. Then wash off the buttermilk and remarinate in wine and herbs if desired.

Ingredients:

2 cups diced Boar pieces
2 diced onions
2 cans Zucchini in Tomato Sauce
2 tsp. Ginger Powder
1 tsp. turmeric
2 tsp. Chili Powder

Directions:

Preheat oven to 350 F
Put all the ingredients except the Cumberland Sauce in an ovenware pot or casserole and cook for 20 minutes

Cumberland Sauce

3/4 cup blackberry jam
1 small box raisins
1 cup Port Wine
2 tbsp. brown Sugar
1 tsp. Corn Starch mixed with 2 ounces of water
2 tsp. Thyme powder
1 tsp. Garlic Powder
1/4 tsp. Ground Cloves

Sauce

Directions

Mix all Ingredients together and simmer until sauce thickens

Grilled Boar With Mushrooms

Important Read This First:

Chef Gahagan says always marinate Wild Boar in Buttermilk and Meat Tenderizer for about three hours. Then wash off the buttermilk and remarinate in wine and herbs if desired.

Ingredients

Boar Chops for 4
1 tbsp. each of tarragon, chives, basil and thyme
1 jar Honey Mustard
1/2 cup olive oil
3 cups chopped mushrooms
1 cup chopped onions
1 tsp. sugar
3/4 cup Chicken Stock salt and pepper to taste

Directons

Mix herbs with chicken stock and 1/4 cup of olive oil. Season and set asides.

Sauté mushrooms, onions and sugar in remaining oil.

Add Chicken Stock and oil seasoning mix and cook two minutes.

Slather Chops with Honey mustard and Warm on grill until done to your taste

Put the Boar chops in the center of the serving plate and top with onion/ mushroom mix.

Easy Grilled Honey Mustard Boar Chops

Important Read This First:

Chef Gahagan says always marinate Wild Boar in Buttermilk and Meat Tenderizer for about three hours. Then wash off the buttermilk and remarinate in wine and herbs if desired.

Ingredients

Easy Grilled Garlic Boar Chops
4, 1/4 lb. Boar Chops
1 tbsp. vegetable oil
2 tsp. Garlic powder
1/4 cup Honey
1/4 cup mustard
1 tsp. Ground Sage
4 cups hot cooked couscous or long-grain white rice

Directions:

Grill or sauté the chops to 140 F. Remove the chops and set aside. Stir the soup, garlic, MSG and milk into the skillet. Heat to a boil. Return the chops to the skillet. Serve with couscous or rice. Serves 4.

Easy Boar Italian Wedding Soup

Important Read This First:

Chef Gahagan says always marinate Wild Boar in Buttermilk and Meat Tenderizer for about three hours. Then wash off the buttermilk and remarinate in wine and herbs if desired.

Ingredients

2 cans Italian Wedding Soup
1 can Italian Stewed Tomatoes
1 1/2 cups diced leftover Boar pieces
2 cups of cooked small Pasta (Shells, Bowties, Rotini, etc.)
2 tsp. Oregano leaves
1 tsp. Garlic powder
1/2 tsp. Pepper
1 tbsp. Parmesan Cheese
1/2 tsp. MSG

Directions

Put all ingredients in a pot, stir and simmer for 6 minutes

Easy Mandarin Boar

Important Read This First:

Chef Gahagan says always marinate Wild Boar in Buttermilk and Meat Tenderizer for about three hours. Then wash off the buttermilk and remarinate in wine and herbs if desired.
8 thin or 4 thick slices of Boar fillet
2 tbsp. butter
1 can drained Mandarin Oranges
4 tbsp. Orange Marmalade
4 tbsp. Slivered Almonds

Directions:

Slice Boar fillet crosswise

Heat Orange Marmalade

Butter a baking pan

Place Boar slices on the pan, overlapping with orange slices in between

Pour Marmalade over chops. Top with slivered Almonds and serve. Do not overcook.

Easy Boar Mustard Mayo

Important Read This First:

Chef Gahagan says always marinate Wild Boar in Buttermilk and Meat Tenderizer for about three hours. Then wash off the buttermilk and remarinate in wine and herbs if desired.

Ingredients

1 pound Thin Sliced Boar
1/2 cup Italian bread crumbs
3 tbsp. Butter
2-3 tbsp. mayonnaise
1 tsp. Oregano
Pinch of salt and pepper
1/2 cup Port Wine
1/2 tsp. MSG

Directions

Put the Boar Slices in a buttered pan.

Spoon the mayonnaise in a thin layer on both sides of boar slices.

Then sprinkle both sides with the bread crumbs, oregano, MSG salt and pepper.

Cover the pan and heat until crusted

Deglaze pan with Port wine and pour over meat.

Easy Mayo Boar Loin

Important Read This First:

Chef Gahagan says always marinate Wild Boar in Buttermilk and Meat Tenderizer for about three hours. Then wash off the buttermilk and remarinate in wine and herbs if desired.

Ingredients:

1 pound Thin Sliced Boar
1/2 cup Italian bread crumbs
3 tbsp. Butter
2-3 tbsp. mayonnaise
1 tsp. Sage
1 tsp. Garlic Powder
1 tsp. sugar
Pinch of salt and pepper
1/2 tsp. MSG

Directions

Mix Bread Crumbs and seasonings, i.e. salt, pepper, sugar, MSG, sage and garlic powder,

Put the Boar Slices in a buttered pan.

Spoon the mayonnaise in a thin layer on both sides of slices.

Then sprinkle both sides with the bread crumbs and seasonings mix.

Cover the pan and heat for 3 minutes or until tender.

Classic Boar Meatloaf

Important Read This First:

Chef Gahagan says always marinate Wild Boar in Buttermilk and Meat Tenderizer for about three hours. Then wash off the buttermilk and remarinate in wine and herbs if desired.
Classic Boar Meatloaf

Ingredients:

1 lb. Ground Beef
1 lb. Ground Boar
1 Forked egg
1 cup cooked Instant Oatmeal
1 tbsp. Sugar
1 medium onion
1 tsp. Garlic Powder
1 tsp. Powdered Sage
Salt and pepper to taste
2 cup Spaghetti Sauce

Directions:

Preheat oven to 350 F

Mix all ingredients except the spaghetti sauce and place in a loaf cooking dish.

Bake at 350 F until done

Heat Spaghetti Sauce and serve in a sauce bowl with the Meat and Onion loaf

German Boar Meatloaf

Important Read This First:

Chef Gahagan says always marinate Wild Boar in Buttermilk and Meat Tenderizer for about three hours. Then wash off the buttermilk and remarinate in wine and herbs if desired.

Ingredients:

1/2 lb. Knockwurst in bite size pieces
1/2 lb. Liverwurst in bite size pieces
1 lb. Ground Boar
1 Forked egg
1 cup Cooked Instant Oatmeal
1 tbsp. Sugar
1 medium onion
1 tsp. Garlic Powder
1 tsp. Powdered Sage
Salt and pepper to taste
2 cup Spaghetti Sauce

Directions:

Preheat oven to 350 F

Mix all ingredients except the spaghetti sauce and place in a loaf cooking dish.

Bake at 350 F until done.

Heat Spaghetti Sauce and serve in a sauce bowl with the Meat and Onion loaf

Italian Boar Meatloaf

Important Read This First:

Chef Gahagan says always marinate Wild Boar in Buttermilk and Meat Tenderizer for about three hours. Then wash off the buttermilk and remarinate in wine and herbs if desired.

Ingredients:

1 lb. Italian Hot Sausage cut into bite size pieces
1 lb. Ground Boar
1 Forked egg
1 cup cooked Instant Oatmeal
1 tbsp. Sugar
1 medium onion
1 tsp. Garlic Powder
Salt and pepper to taste
2 cup Spaghetti Sauce

Directions:

Preheat oven to 350 F

Mix all ingredients except the spaghetti sauce and place in a loaf cooking dish.

Bake at 350 F until done.

Heat Spaghetti Sauce and serve in a sauce bowl with the Meat and Onion loaf

Spanish Boar Meatloaf

Important Read This First:

Chef Gahagan says always marinate Wild Boar in Buttermilk and Meat Tenderizer for about three hours. Then wash off the buttermilk and remarinate in wine and herbs if desired.

Ingredients:

1 lb. Chorizo Sausage cut into bite size pieces
1 lb. Ground Boar
1 Forked egg
1 cup cooked Instant Oatmeal
1 tbsp. Sugar
1 medium onion
1 tsp. Garlic Powder
1 tsp. Powdered Sage
2 tsp. Salt
2 tsp. Chili pepper to taste
2 cup Spaghetti Sauce

Directions:

Preheat oven to 350 F

Mix all ingredients except the spaghetti sauce and place in a loaf cooking dish.

Bake at 350 F until done.

Heat Spaghetti Sauce and serve in a sauce bowl with the Meat and Onion loaf

Polish Boar Meatloaf

Important Read This First:

Chef Gahagan says always marinate Wild Boar in Buttermilk and Meat Tenderizer for about three hours. Then wash off the buttermilk and remarinate in wine and herbs if desired.

Ingredients:

1 lb. Kielb.asa cut into bite size pieces
1 lb. Ground Boar
1 Forked egg
1 cup cooked Instant Oatmeal
1 tbsp. Sugar
1 medium onion
1 tsp. Garlic Powder
1 tsp. Powdered Sage
Salt and pepper to taste
2 cup Spaghetti Sauce

Directions:

Preheat oven to 350 F

Mix all ingredients except the spaghetti sauce and place in a loaf cooking dish.

Bake at 350 F until done.

Heat Spaghetti Sauce and serve in a sauce bowl with the Meat and Onion loaf

Mexican Boar

Important Read This First:

Chef Gahagan says always marinate Wild Boar in Buttermilk and Meat Tenderizer for about three hours. Then wash off the buttermilk and remarinate in wine and herbs if desired.

Ingredients

2 cups diced Boar
4 tbsp. butter
8 tbsp. Salsa (your choice of "hot")
1 tbsp. Dark Rum
Shredded Cheddar or Monterey Jack Cheese

Directions:

Scissor Boar into bite size pieces.

Warm Boar and butter in a pot, Stirring occasionally so it does not stick together.

Add salsa, top with Cheddar or Monterey Jack and rum when Boar is almost done.

Easy Boar with Mushrooms

Important Read This First:

Chef Gahagan says always marinate Wild Boar in Buttermilk and Meat Tenderizer for about three hours. Then wash off the buttermilk and remarinate in wine and herbs if desired.

Ingredients

Boar Chops for 4
1 tbsp. each of tarragon, chives, basil and thyme
1/4 cup olive oil
2 cups chopped mushrooms
1 cup chopped onions
1 tsp. sugar
3/4 cup Chicken Stock
Salt and Pepper to taste

Directions

Mix herbs with 3/4 cup of chicken stock. Season and set aside to soak

Sauté mushrooms, onions and sugar in oil.

Add Chicken Stock and seasoning mix and cook two minutes.

Grill, broil or sauté Boar Chops until tender

Put onion/mushroom mix in the center of plate with the Boar on top.

Boar Rice Bake

Important Read This First:

Chef Gahagan says always marinate Wild Boar in Buttermilk and Meat Tenderizer for about three hours. Then wash off the buttermilk and remarinate in wine and herbs if desired.

2 lbs. Boar, cut up
12 baby carrots
1 pkg. Onion Soup Mix
1 Cup Uncooked Rice
Can Cream of Chicken Soup
1 Can of Milk
1/2 tsp. pepper
1 Can French Fried Onion Rings
1 tsp. MSG

Directions

Simmer Boar and carrots in water.

Sprinkle MSG and dry soup mix into buttered Casserole dish; Sprinkle rice over soup mix; Add cooked Boar pieces Pour Soup and milk mixture over Boar.

Cover and bake 350 degree oven 1 hr and 15 minutes. Uncover a sprinkle with onion rings. Cook 15 minutes longer.

Add water as necessary. Check to adjust seasonings.

Boar in White Wine and Orange

Important Read This First:

Chef Gahagan says always marinate Wild Boar in Buttermilk and Meat Tenderizer for about three hours. Then wash off the buttermilk and remarinate in wine and herbs if desired.

Ingredients

6-8 thin slices of Boar loin
2 tsp. Dill
2 cups white wine
8 orange sections
2 tbsp. Orange Marmalade
2 tbsp. sugar
Salt and pepper to taste

Directions

Put all ingredients in a pot and simmer until Boar is very tender.

Place Boar on a serving plate and overlap the pieces with orange sections.

Top with marmalade

Boar Paprika

Important Read This First:

Chef Gahagan says always marinate Wild Boar in Buttermilk and Meat Tenderizer for about three hours. Then wash off the buttermilk and remarinate in wine and herbs if desired.

Ingredients

12 slices bacon, cut up
1/2 cup chopped onion
1 1/2 tsp. paprika
1 1/2 tsp. salt
2-3 lbs. Boar pieces
1 can Chicken Soup/stock
1 can cream of Chicken Soup
3 tbsp. Paprika

Directions

In medium size skillet, gently cook bacon until it is crisp Remove Bacon and reserve. Add onion. Cook and stir until onion is tender. Remove from heat. Remove bacon and onion from skillet; set asides; reserve drippings.

Add 1 cup Chicken stock to pan. Reduce heat; cover. Simmer until tender.

Mix milk, Cream of Chicken Soup and 1 tbsp. paprika and add to skillet.

Preheat to serving temperature and top with remaining paprika.
Serve with egg noodles.

Boar Parisian

Important Read This First:

Chef Gahagan says always marinate Wild Boar in Buttermilk and Meat Tenderizer for about three hours. Then wash off the buttermilk and remarinate in wine and herbs if desired.
Chef's Note: This is a famous French dish. They call Clarified Butter Buerre Blanc and it makes one of the great sauces of the world. It is so simple that you will not believe how good it can be.

Ingredients

A 6 slice size of Boar Tenderloin
1 cup butter salt and pepper

Directions:

Heat butter to foaming and skim off the scum until the butter is clear

Roast Boar tenderloin to 140 F on a meat thermometer or sauté to the degree of rareness you like.

Cover with Clarified Butter sauce

Easy Boar Parmesan

Important Read This First:

Chef Gahagan says always marinate Wild Boar in Buttermilk and Meat Tenderizer for about three hours. Then wash off the buttermilk and remarinate in wine and herbs if desired.

Ingredients

2 pounds Boar in bite size pieces
4 tbsp. Butter
1 cup bread crumbs
1 cup sliced mozzarella
1/2 cup grated Parmesan cheese
2 tsp. garlic powder
2 tbsp. Olive oil
1 tbsp. Oregano
1 cup sliced onions
1 cup Port wine

Directions

Cover Boar pieces with melted butter.

Dredge buttered Boar in a mixture of bread crumbs, oregano, garlic powder and 2/3 of the parmesan cheese

Arrange Boar in a Casserole. Add butter. Top with onion slices and then Mozzarella. Add remaining butter and Parmesan Cheese. Cover with foil and Casserole dish top

Bake into a preheated 350 F oven until Boar is tender. Check to see if moisture is needed. If so, add Port wine or water.

Boar with Peaches and Rum

Important Read This First:

Chef Gahagan says always marinate Wild Boar in Buttermilk and Meat Tenderizer for about three hours. Then wash off the buttermilk and remarinate in wine and herbs if desired.

Ingredients:

8 thin slices of Boar Loin
2 forked eggs
4 tbsp. butter
1 small can sliced peaches
2 ounces Dark Rum
Salt and Pepper to taste

Directions:

Drain Can of Peaches add rum and blend to make a sauce

Dip Boar s in forked eggs

Sauté until done Cover with peach sauce Heat gently and serve

Easy Boar Pecan

Important Read This First:

Chef Gahagan says always marinate Wild Boar in Buttermilk and Meat Tenderizer for about three hours. Then wash off the buttermilk and remarinate in wine and herbs if desired.

Ingredients

4 Boar Chops
4 tbsp. butter
4 ounces (125 g) Pecan bits
1/2 cup honey
3 tbsp. water
Salt and pepper to taste
1/2 cup Port Wine

Directions

Chop Pecan bits in food processor or blender

Saute Pecans in 1 tbsp. butter

Remove Pecans, add the rest of the butter and gentley sauté Boar Chops t0 140 F, turning so both sides are coated with butter and Pecan bits.

Add the honey back into the pan, add water and stir together.

Put the Boar on a serving plate. Then deglaze the pan with Port wine and pour the Pecan, Honey/Butter/Port wine sauce over the Boar Chops.

Easy Peanut Maple Boar

Important Read This First:

Chef Gahagan says always marinate Wild Boar in Buttermilk and Meat Tenderizer for about three hours. Then wash off the buttermilk and remarinate in wine and herbs if desired.

Ingredients

4 fresh Boar Chops
4 tbsp. s butter
4 ounces (125g) Unsalted Peanuts
1/2 cup Maple Syrup
Salt and pepper to taste

Directions

Chop peanuts in Blender of food processor. Then sauté Peanuts in 1 tbsp. Butter, Remove Peanuts to a medium size bowl.

Add the rest of the butter to the pan and sauté Boar Chops until done.

Then put the Boar Chops on a serving dish.

Add the maple syrup and the peanuts to the pan and stir together until hot. Then deglaze the pan and pour the Peanut/Maple Syrup/Butter sauce over the Boar Chops.

Boar in Plum Sauce

Important Read This First:

Chef Gahagan says always marinate Wild Boar in Buttermilk and Meat Tenderizer for about three hours. Then wash off the buttermilk and remarinate in wine and herbs if desired.

Ingredients

2 cups of Boar loins cut into bite size pieces
1/2 cup melted Butter
Paprika for color
1 can Plums
1 cup Heavy Cream
1/2 tsp. MSG

Directions

First prepare the Plum Sauce.

Drain Plums, remove any pits and puree with cream and MSG on high.

Then, slowly simmer until thickened.

The Boar

Sprinkle Boar pieces with paprika, place them in a skillet with melted butter and mix.

Place them in a Casserole dish and top with Plum Cream Sauce. Decorate

Easy Boar Portobello

Important Read This First:

Chef Gahagan says always marinate Wild Boar in Buttermilk and Meat Tenderizer for about three hours. Then wash off the buttermilk and remarinate in wine and herbs if desired.

Ingredients

6 Boar Chops or pieces of Boar Loin
6 tbsp. butter
1 sliced Portobello Mushroom
1 can mushroom soup
6 ounces Light Cream
1/2 tsp. MSG

Directions:

Heat Boar in 4 tbsp. Butter until tender.

Remove Boar from pan and put in a Casserole dish.

Chop Mushroom in a blender or food processor, put in the pan and sauté in remaining butter.

Next, mix in Light Cream, MSG and Mushroom Soup to make a sauce.

Pour the sauce over the Boar, heat and serve.

Easy Boar Provencal

Important Read This First:

Chef Gahagan says always marinate Wild Boar in Buttermilk and Meat Tenderizer for about three hours. Then wash off the buttermilk and remarinate in wine and herbs if desired.

Ingredients

3 cups Boar loin leftovers or Pulled Boar Pieces
1 can Italian Stewed tomatoes
1 can Chicken Broth or stock
8 carrots
1 chopped onion
1/2 cup chopped celery
1/2 cup parmesan cheese
2 tsp. Garlic powder
1/2 tsp. MSG
2 tsp. Sugar (tomatoes are acidic)
Salt and pepper to taste

Directions

Put all vegetables and seasonings in a casserole and simmer

When vegetables are tender, add boar, cover with Mozzarella cheese and top with Parmesan.

Easy Grilled Honey Mustard Boar Chops

Important Read This First:

Chef Gahagan says always marinate Wild Boar in Buttermilk and Meat Tenderizer for about three hours. Then wash off the buttermilk and remarinate in wine and herbs if desired.

Ingredients

Boar Chops for 4 to 6 people
1 jar Honey Mustard
1/2 cup olive oil
3 cups chopped mushrooms
1 cup chopped onions
1 tsp. sugar salt and pepper to taste

Directons

Mix herbs with 1/4 cup of olive oil. Season and set aside.

Oil Boar Chops/Loin slices and Grill to 140 F.

Sauté mushrooms, onions and sugar in remaining oil.

Slather Chops with Honey mustard and Grill until done to your taste

Put The Boar chops in the center of serving dish and cover with onion and mushroom mix

Easy Honey Baked Boar

Important Read This First:

Chef Gahagan says always marinate Wild Boar in Buttermilk and Meat Tenderizer for about three hours. Then wash off the buttermilk and remarinate in wine and herbs if desired.

Ingredients

6 Boar Chops
1 1/2 tsp. Onion Powder
1 tsp. Garlic powder
1 tsp. MSG
1 tbsp. paprika
1 cup honey
1 cup butter salt and pepper to taste
4 tbsp. Olive oil

Directions

Preheat oven to 325 F.

Gently sauté Boar to 140 F.

Mix honey, butter and seasonings.

Put Boar Chops in a Casserole dish. Cover with the honey/butter mixture and bake until warm throughout.

Easy Italian Boar Casserole

Important Read This First:

Chef Gahagan says always marinate Wild Boar in Buttermilk and Meat Tenderizer for about three hours. Then wash off the buttermilk and remarinate in wine and herbs if desired.

Ingredients

1 lb. Boar or Boar leftovers chopped medium onion
1 green pepper
1/2 tsp. garlic powder
1/4 cup olive oil
1 jar your favorite spaghetti sauce
1 cup Mozzarella cheese
1/2 cup Parmesan cheese
1 tbsp. sugar
1 tsp. oregano salt and pepper to taste

Mix vegetables and seasonings and cook until tender.

Pour off water. Add Boar and Spaghetti Sauce, top with Mozzarella and the Parmesan cheeses.

Heat until Cheese melts and serve with rice or pasta

Easy Tijuana Boar Stew

Important Read This First:

Chef Gahagan says always marinate Wild Boar in Buttermilk and Meat Tenderizer for about three hours. Then wash off the buttermilk and remarinate in wine and herbs if desired.

Ingredients

4 cups cooked small Pasta (shells, Twists, etc.)
1 cup pasta sauce
2 tbsp. olive oil
2 jars Salsa (your choice of hot)
2 lbs. Ground Boar
1 package Shredded Monterey Jack Cheese

Directions:

Put all ingredients except Monterey Jack Cheese in a Casserole and mix thoroughly. Sprinkle cheese on top and bake for 25 minutes @ 350 F

Easy Vesuvious Boar

Important Read This First:

Chef Gahagan says always marinate Wild Boar in Buttermilk and Meat Tenderizer for about three hours. Then wash off the buttermilk and remarinate in wine and herbs if desired.

Ingredients

2 lbs. Boar leftovers
1 jar hot Salsa sauce
1 jar Pasta Sauce
1 tsp. Garlic Powder
1 tsp. Oregano Powder
1 pkg. Shredded Mozzarella cheese

Directions

Mix all ingredients together, cook until hot, top with Mozzarella and serve

Roast Boar Cream Sherry Sauce

Important Read This First:

Chef Gahagan says always marinate Wild Boar in Buttermilk and Meat Tenderizer for about three hours. Then wash off the buttermilk and remarinate in wine and herbs if desired.

Ingredients

4-5 lbs. Boar Roast
Salt and pepper to taste
6 bacon slices
1 can/cup meat stock
1/2 cup Sherry
One half cup heavy cream
Seedless Grapes
Cooked rice

Directions

Sprinkle salt and pepper on Boar. Roast at 350 F to 140 F on the meat thermometer.

When done, remove the Boar from the pan. Deglaze pan and pour off the fat. Add cream and Sherry and stir into a sauce. Add grapes to the sauce to decorate.

Serve with rice.

Pulled Boar

Important Read This First:

Chef Gahagan says always marinate Wild Boar in Buttermilk and Meat Tenderizer for about three hours. Then wash off the buttermilk and remarinate in wine and herbs if desired.
Our Chef says: This classic American dish is messy and time consuming to fix but it will feed you forever and is a delicious to eat.

Ingredients

1 lb. Boar Shoulder
1 bottle your favorite Barbecue Sauce
Hamburger Rolls

Directions

Roast Boar shoulder for 6-8 hours in a 200 F oven.

Cut open the shoulder. Pull out the meat, scissor it into bite size pieces and place it in a large bowl,

Use what you need. Refrigerate what you will need in the near future and freeze the rest for Casseroles, stews and other dishes.

Put the bones, scraps and skin in a pot, cover with water and cook for 3 more hours on low to make a Boar stock. Taste to determine how much salt is needed. Add more water if needed.

Classic Boar Hamburger

Ingredients:

1 lb. Ground Beef
1 lb. Ground Boar
1 tsp. Sugar
1 tsp. Garlic Powder
Salt and pepper to taste

Directions:

Ingredients:

1 lb. Kielb.asa cut into bite size pieces
1 lb. Ground Boar
1 tsp. Sugar
1 tsp. Garlic Powder
Salt and pepper to taste

Directions:

Mix all ingredients into patties and saute or wrap and freeze

German Boar Hamburger

Important Read This First:

Chef Gahagan says always marinate Wild Boar in Buttermilk and Meat Tenderizer for about three hours. Then wash off the buttermilk and remarinate in wine and herbs if desired.

Ingredients:

1/2 lb. Knockwurst in bite size pieces
1/2 lb. Liverwurst in bite size pieces
1 lb. Ground Boar
1 tsp. Sugar
1 medium onion
1 tsp. Garlic Powder
1 tsp. Powdered Sage
Salt and pepper to taste

Directions:

Ingredients:

1 lb. Kielb.asa cut into bite size pieces
1 lb. Ground Boar
1 tsp. Sugar
1 tsp. Garlic Powder
Salt and pepper to taste

Directions:

Mix all ingredients into patties and saute or wrap and freeze

Italian Boar Meatloaf

Important Read This First:

Chef Gahagan says always marinate Wild Boar in Buttermilk and Meat Tenderizer for about three hours. Then wash off the buttermilk and remarinate in wine and herbs if desired.

Ingredients:

1 lb. Italian Hot Sausage cut into bite size pieces
1 lb. Ground Boar
1 tsp. Sugar
1 tsp. Garlic Powder
Salt and pepper to taste

Directions:

Ingredients:

1 lb. Kielb.asa cut into bite size pieces
1 lb. Ground Boar
1 tsp. Sugar
1 tsp. Garlic Powder
Salt and pepper to taste

Directions:

Mix all ingredients into patties and saute or wrap and freeze

Spanish Boar Hamburger

Important Read This First:

Chef Gahagan says always marinate Wild Boar in Buttermilk and Meat Tenderizer for about three hours. Then wash off the buttermilk and remarinate in wine and herbs if desired.

Ingredients:

1 lb. Chorizo Sausage cut into bite size pieces
1 lb. Ground Boar
1 tsp. Sugar
1 tsp. Garlic Powder
1 tsp. Powdered Sage
2 tsp. Salt
2 tsp. Chili pepper to taste

Directions:

Mix all ingredients into patties and saute or wrap and freeze

Polish Boar Hamburger

Important Read This First:

Chef Gahagan says always marinate Wild Boar in Buttermilk and Meat Tenderizer for about three hours. Then wash off the buttermilk and remarinate in wine and herbs if desired.

Ingredients:

1 lb. Kielb.asa cut into bite size pieces
1 lb. Ground Boar
1 tsp. Sugar
1 tsp. Garlic Powder
Salt and pepper to taste

Directions:

Mix all ingredients into patties and saute or wrap and freeze

Boar in Honey Cream Sauce

Two lbs. Boar meat cleaned and cut into bite size pieces
One 1/2 cup sherry
1/2 cup oil
2 garlic cloves, crushed
1/4 cup butter
Salt and pepper to taste
1/2 tsp. thyme
1/2 tsp. rosemary
1 med. onion, sliced thin
1 1/4 cups heavy cream
1 tbsp. sugar

Mix sherry, oil, garlic and sugar to form a marinade and add Boar.

Marinate about 8 hrs. turning meat occasionally. If the boar is tough, sprinkle in some meat tenderizer. Remove Boar and reserve marinade.

Melt butter in deep skillet and brown Boar pieces. Pour in marinade and bring to a boil. Stir in seasoning, cover and simmer until tender (about 1-1 1/4 hours.) Remove skillet from the fire and place Boar pieces on a warmed platter.

Mix mustard and cornstarch, then mix in cream. Return skillet to low heat and stir in this mixture a little at a time. Stir sauce until hot, but not boiling, and thickened. Pour sauce over Boar. Serve with steamed rice.

Apricot Boar Boar Tenderloin Boar Stew

1 lb. Boar tenderloin
1/2 tsp. ground thyme
1/4 tsp. ground nutmeg
1 tsp. black pepper
1/2 tsp. sugar
1 cup hickory chips
5 lb. of charcoal
Blackberry Sauce
parsley sprigs
artichoke hearts
yellow squash slices

Mix thyme, nutmeg, pepper and soy sauce, and marinate Boar tenderloin overnight in the refrigerator. Soak 1 cup of hickory chips in a bucket of water overnight.

Build a fire in a covered barbecue grill using 5 lbs. of charcoal. Allow the coals to burn for 30 minutes. If using a gas grill, preheat for 30 minutes.

Scatter the soaked chips over the coals and close the lid for 10 minutes. Place the tenderloin on the grill and baste with the marinade, Close the lid and cook for 5 minutes. Turn the tenderloin and baste again.

Close the lid and cook for another 5 minutes. The meat should be rare because game has no fat and boar in articular toughens quickly. Serve on a platter with Blackberry Sauce. Garnish with parsley sprigs, artichoke hearts and yellow squash slices. Serves 2 to 4.

Boar Steaks Flamed in Marmalade

Important Read This First:

Chef Gahagan says always marinate Wild Boar in Buttermilk and Meat Tenderizer for about three hours. Then wash off the buttermilk and remarinate in wine and herbs if desired.
4 Wild Boar Loin Steaks
1 ounce brandy
One half tsp. Garlic powder
1 cup orange marmelade salt and pepper
2 tbsp. of bacon fat
1 tsp.dry mustard

Directions

Slice the steaks and beat them so that they are thin. Salt and Pepper the steaks and sprinkle with dry mustard. Saute them quickly in the oil and lay them in a dish garnished with paper thin slices of orange, brush marmalade over the steaks. Detach the glaze from the flying pan with a little water. Whe you serve, warm the brandy in a small pot, ignite it and pour it over the pan juices and give them a gentle stir and tip the flaming sauce over the steaks.

Roast Boar

Important Read This First:

Chef Gahagan says always marinate Wild Boar in Buttermilk and Meat Tenderizer for about three hours. Then wash off the buttermilk and remarinate in wine and herbs if desired.
4-5 Lb. Boar Roast
1 onw half cups chopped onion
1 one half cups chopped carrots
1 cup chopped celery salt and pepper garlic to taste
2 tbsp. of bacon fat
1 tsp. powdered sage
Salt and pepper
1 tsp. msg.
1 cup red wine
1 tbsp. sugar

Directions

Put all the ingredients in your pot, cover with water and cook until tender.

Remove vegetables and blend on high. Remove Roast and put on serving plate. Return vegetables to pot and adjust seasonings and thickness. Pour over meat, garnish plate with fresh slice vegetables and serve.

DOVE RECIPES

Dove Amandine

6 woodcock, or 12 Dove or snipe split down back
1/4 cup flour
Salt and pepper
4 tbsp. butter
1/2 cup white table wine
2 tbsp. lemon juice
1/4 cup blanched, sliced almonds

Dust birds in flour seasoned with salt and pepper. Melt butter in a heavy skillet or electric frying pan and saute birds until nicely browned. Add wine and lemon juice. Cover and continue cooking slowly for 15-20 minutes.

Add almonds and cook for 5-10 minutes longer or until birds are fork tender. (Allow 2 quail or woodcock per serving; 4 Dove or snipe.)

Dove Roast

6 woodcock, or 12 Dove or snipe split down back
1/4 cup flour
Salt and pepper
4 tbsp. butter
1 1/2 cup red table wine
2 tbsp. lemon juice
1/4 cup blanched, sliced almonds

Dust birds in flour seasoned with salt and pepper. Melt butter in a heavy skillet or electric frying pan and saute birds until nicely browned. Add wine and lemon juice. Cover and continue cooking slowly for 15-20 minutes.

Add almonds and cook for 5-10 minutes longer or until birds are fork tender. (Allow 2 quail or woodcock per serving; 4 Dove or snipe.)

Dove Casserole

3 lbs. quail or Dove
1 1/2 tsp. salt
1/2 tsp. pepper
1/2 tsp. paprika
6 tbsp. butter
15 oz. can artichokes
1/4 lb. mushrooms
2 tbsp. flour
2/3 cup chicken consomme
3-4 tbsp. sherry (cream or cooking)

Salt, pepper, and paprika quail or Dove and fry in 4 tbsp. butter. Place in casserole. Place artichokes between quail or Dove. Saute mushrooms in 2 tbsp. butter. Add 2 tbsp. flour. Stir in consomme and sherry. Cook 5 minutes. Pour over quail or Dove. Cover and cook at 350 degrees for 1 hour.

Dove with Artichokes

3 lbs. quail or Dove
1 1/2 tsp. salt
1/2 tsp. pepper
1/2 tsp. paprika
6 tbsp. butter
15 oz. can artichokes
1/4 lb. mushrooms
2 tbsp. flour
2/3 cup chicken consomme
3-4 tbsp. sherry (cream or cooking)

Salt, pepper, and paprika quail or Dove and fry in 4 tbsp. butter. Place in casserole. Place artichokes between quail or Dove. Saute mushrooms in 2 tbsp. butter. Add 2 tbsp. flour. Stir in consomme and sherry. Cook 5 minutes. Pour over quail or Dove. Cover and cook at 350 degrees for 1 hour. Correct seasonings

Dove Sherry Roast

8 Doves
1/2 cup flour
2 tsp. salt
1/2 tsp. pepper
1/2 cup cooking oil
1/3 cup green onion, chopped
2 stalks chopped celery 1 cup water
1/2 cup sherry parsley to garnish

Split Doves and cover them in flour, salt, and pepper mixture. Heat cooking oil to 350 degrees and braise Doves lightly. Place Doves and excess cooking oil in roasting pan with cover and add chopped onion and water. Bake at 350 degrees until tender. Baste often and add sherry during final minutes of cooking. Add parsley as garnish. 4-6 servings.

Baked Dove

12-18 quail or Dove breasts
1 med. onion, chopped
2 tbsp. melted butter or margarine
Salt and pepper
1 can cream of celery soup—undiluted
1/2 tsp. oregano
1 (4 oz.) can mushrooms, drained
1/2 tsp. rosemary
1/2 cup Sauterne (white wine)
1 cup sour cream
Cooked wild rice

Arrange quail in a large baking dish—do not crowd. Saute onion in butter, add remaining ingredients except sour cream and rice. Pour over quail and cover dish. Bake at 325 degrees for 1 hour, turning quail occasionally.

Add sour cream and stir into sauce. Leave uncovered and bake an additional 20 minutes. Spoon sauce over rice.

Dove in Sherry

8 Doves
1/2 cup flour
2 tsp. salt
1/2 tsp. pepper
1/2 cup cooking oil
1/3 cup green onion, chopped
1 cup water
1/2 cup sherry parsley to garnish

Split Doves and dredge in flour, salt, and pepper mixture. Heat cooking oil to 350 degrees and braise Doves lightly. Place Doves and excess cooking oil in roastingpan with cover and add chopped onion and water. Bake at 350 degrees for 45 minutes or until tender. Baste often and add sherry during final minutes of cooking. Add parsley as garnish. 4-6 servings.

Parmesan Dove

12 Doves
Salt and pepper
Flour
1/3 cup butter or margarine
1 small onion, chopped
2 carrots, chopped
Fresh parsley, chopped (or parsley flakes)
1 cup chicken broth or chicken bouillon
1/2 cup parmesan
1/2 cup dry white wine

Preheat oven to 350 degrees F. Split Doves down the back, add salt and pepper to flour; dust birds lightly with flour mixture. Melt butter in heavy skillet and place the birds in pan breast side down. Saute, turning birds oftenuntil browned on both sides. Remove birds from skillet and place them in a casserole dish with lid. Pour drippings from skillet over birds; add onions, carrots, parsley, chicken broth, and wine. Cover dish and bake birds for 45 minutes.

Spoon wine gravy over the birds when serving. Serves 4-5 people.

Barbecued Dove

Split birds down the back. Dust lightly with flour and Saute in bacon fat.

Brown quickly on skin side; turn and cook on bone side and turn again.

Reduce heat and continue cooking until birds are tender.

Depending on size and number of birds, cooking will take from 15-20 minutes. Season birds with salt and pepper to taste. Remove birds from skillet and add 1/2 cup of dry wine to drippings. Bring to boil to deglaze the pan and serve as clear gravy.

Dove Breasts

12-18 breasts
1 diced medium onion
1 can cream of mushroom soup
1/4 to 1/2 cup sherry
Pinch of oregano
Pinch of crushed rosemary
Salt and pepper to taste
1/2 pint sour cream
Clean birds according to

Directions

Place breasts meaty side down in 15X12 inch baking dish. Do not over-crowd. Saute onions in small amount of fat in skillet. Mix onion, sherry, herbs, salt, and pepper. Pour over bird breasts. Cover baking dish lightly with foil. Bake in 325 degree F. oven for 1 hour, turning occasionally. Add sour cream. Stir, bake about 20 minutes longer.

Dove in Wild Rice

8 to 10 Dove breasts
1 box wild rice
1 can cream of chicken soup
1 can cream of celery soup
1 can milk
1 can water
Onion, chopped
Salt
Pepper
Clean birds according to

Directions

Mix all ingredients in casserole pan and lay Dove breasts on top of mixture.

Cover with aluminum foil and bake 2 to 2 1/2 hours at 325 degrees F.

Gumbo Dove Breasts

Ten Dove breasts
Seasoned salt
Pepper
Flour
Cooking Oil
1 can chicken gumbo soup
1 can golden mushroom soup
1 can onion soup

Preheat oven to 350 degrees F. Sprinkle seasoned salt and pepper on quail breasts and flour them. Brown lightly in a skillet with cooking oil; then put in a greased baking dish and set aside. Combine the 3 cans of soup in a saucepan and heat. Pour soup mixture over quail and bake 1 hour.

Also good with Dove and pheasant.

Dove w Piquant Sauce

10 Dove breast fillets
1/4 cup flour
1/2 tsp. garlic salt
1/4 tsp. paprika
1/8 tsp. pepper
2 tbsp. bacon fat
Clean birds according to

Directons

Place flour, garlic salt, paprika, and pepper in a plastic or paper bag; add Dove breasts and shake until meat is well coated. Heat bacon fat in medium skillet and brown breasts on both sides. Remove meat to platter and keep warm while preparing sauce.

PIQUANT SAUCE:

1 med. onion, sliced
1 tbsp. bacon fat
2/3 cup water
2 tsp. cornstarch
2 tsp. soy sauce

Cook and stir onion until crisp-tender in same skillet used for Doves.

Blend water, cornstarch and soy sauce and pour into skillet. Cook and stir constantly until sauce thickens and boils. Continue stirring and allow to boil for one minute. Add Doves to sauce, heat through, and serve on bed of cooked rice.

Dove and Beans

Three lbs. dry kidney or pinto beans, cooked
OR 64 oz. canned beans
30 oz. stewed tomatoes, undrained
4 oz. canned diced jalapenos (more or less to taste)
1 large red onion, chunked
1 tsp. garlic powder
Dash salt
1 lb. ground beef, browned and drained
*1/2 lb. rattlesnake meat, cut into bite-size pieces
Broken tortilla chips

*(If desired, substitute for rattler: quail, Dove, chicken, rabbit, or pork) Put cooked beans into large pot; add tomatoes, jalapenos, onion, salt, garlic, ground beef, and rattlesnak (or other meat). Simmer 10 minutes to heat thoroughly. For chili pie, put broken tortilla chips in bottom of bowl and spoon beans over chips.

Dove Tetrazini

1 1/2 cups boned Doves
3 tbsp. butter or margarine
3 tbsp. onion, chopped
1/3 cup mushrooms, sliced
1 1/2 cups Dove broth
2 tbsp. cornstarch
2 cups thin spaghetti
1 cup parmesan cheese
1/2 cup crumbled, crisp bacon
Clean birds according to

Directions

Melt butter in saucepan; cook onions and mushrooms over low heat until tender. Add Dove broth and cornstarch and stir until thickened. Add Dove and spaghetti. Heat mixture until bubbling, stirring frequently. Turn into baking dish and top with parmesan cheese and bacon. Place under broiler until cheese melts.

Baked Dove Breasts

10 quail breasts
Seasoned salt
Pepper
Flour
Cooking Oil
1 can chicken gumbo soup
1 can golden mushroom soup
1 can onion soup

Preheat oven to 350 degrees F. Sprinkle seasoned salt and pepper on quail breasts and flour them. Brown lightly in a skillet with cooking oil; then put in a greasedbaking dish and set aside. Combine the 3 cans of soup in a saucepan and heat. Pour soup mixture over quail and bake 1 hour.

Also good with Dove and pheasant.

Dove Mexican Style

1 bag dry kidney or pinto beans, cooked
30 oz. stewed tomatoes, undrained
4 oz. canned diced jalapenos (more or less to taste)
1 large red onion, chunked
1 tsp. garlic powder
Dash salt
1 lb. ground beef, browned and drained
*1/2 lb. rattlesnake meat, cut into bite-size pieces
Broken tortilla chips

*(If desired, substitute for rattler: quail, Dove, chicken, rabbit, or pork) Put cooked beans into large pot; add tomatoes, jalapenos, onion, salt, garlic, ground beef,. Simmer 10 minutes to heat thoroughly. For chili pie, put broken tortilla chips in bottom of bowl and spoon beans over chips.

Dove Cassoulet

3 lbs. dry great northern beans, cooked
15 oz. stewed tomatoes, undrained one quart of chicken stock
10 baby carrots
2 celery stalks chopped
1 large onion, chunked
2 garlic cloves pepper salt
1/2 lb. Italian sweet3 sausage crumbled
2 tblsp sugar

*(If desired, substitute for rattler: quail, Dove, Turkey, rabbit, or pork) Put cooked beans into large pot; add tomatoes, onion, celery, carrots salt, garlic, sugar, sausage,. Simmer 25 minutes to heat thoroughly.

DUCK RECIPES

about roasting Duck

Wash bird well. Then marinate in buttermilk to tenderize the meat and get rid of the strong flavor. Stuff Duck with apple, orange, celery, and onion. You may cook the birds slowly at 350 degrees F or quickly at 450 degrees F. Be sure to baste often with a mixture of butter and wine or butter and broth. The time required will depend on the size of the bird and the desired amount of doneness. Geese will require 20-30 minutes at 450 degrees F. and 1 to 1 1/2 hours at 350 degrees F. A Duck will take 15-30 minutes longer than a Duck.

As a general rule, the bird is done when the leg can be moved back and forth easily. Wild Duck and geese have less fat than domestic varieties and do not create as much mess in the oven.

Duck or Duck can also be cooked in a bag with seasonings. At 350 degrees F, Duck will take about 1 1/2 hours. Plan on 2 hours cooking time for a Duck in a bag.

A large Duck will feed 2 people, a smaller Duck or a teal will feed 1 person. A 6 lb. dressed Duck will feed 4 to 6 people.

Stewed Duck

Ingredients

1 Duck or 2 Ducks, cut up
I can zucchini in tomato sauce
Salt and pepper
2 apple, cut into wedges
15 baby carrots
5 small potatoes
2 Cut up celery stalks
2 tbsp. Bacon drippings
1 tbsp. sugar
Water
1 cup Port Wine

Combine all ingredients in a pot. Cover with wine and water and cook until tender. Discard apple.

Baked Duck

Ingredients

4 Ducks
Salt, pepper
1 tbsp. Sugar
1 tbsp. cinnamon
1 tbsp. ginger
1 cup Italian Salad derssing
3/4 cup cooking sherry

Directions

Thoroughly wash and rinse Duck
Sprinkle salt, pepper, sugar, ginger and cinnamon over entire Duck. Rub into skin. Combine 1/2 thr sherry with the rest of the seasonings and pour over Duck. Bake for 1 hour @ 350 degrees with top on roasting pan. Take top off; broil 8 minutes. Turn Duck breast side up and broil 8 minutes.

SAUCE: Deglaze pan with sherry, pour off any fat and add flour to make a wine sauce. Pour over thinly sliced Duck.

Stuffed Duck

Ingredients

4 wild Ducks
Giblets from Duck
4 cups bread crumbs
2 medium. onions
2 apples, diced
1/4 tsp. sage
1 tsp. garlic powder
2 tsp. salt
1 tsp. pepper
1 tbsp. sugar
1 cup sherry

Directions

Place Duck in roasting pan and roast for about 20 minutes per pound of Duck at 350 degrees. Baste often.

Cook giblets until tender; reserve liquid. Chop giblets and add to bread crumbs, onions, apples, and seasonings. Add liquid from giblets to moisten stuffing.

Pour off fat. Deglaze pan with sherry. Add some salt and pepper to correct seasonings. This makes 6-8 servings.

Duck with Sauerkraut

Ingredients

2 Duck quartered and washed
1 tbsp. salt
2 tsp. Chili powder
1 tsp. garlic
1 apples, quartered
1 onion, quartered
4 slices of bacon
2 cups water
3 cups canned sauerkraut
1 tsp. caraway seeds
2 tbsp. Brown sugar
4 slices well done bacon

Directions

Preheat oven to 350 F.

Season Geese with mixture of salt, chili powder, and garlic. Quarter apples and onions and stuff half into bird cavities. Cover breasts with uncooked bacon and place into baking pan. Place pan in preheated 350 degrees F. oven; bake 3 hours. Baste every 30 minutes.

Soak sau1 1erkraut in water twice. It is very salty. Then combine sauerkraut, caraway seeds, crumbled bacon and brown sugar in a covered pot. Mix well. Simmer for 1 and a half hours on low, adding water as needed. Place in oven 20 minutes before Ducks are done.

Serve quartered Duck or Ducks on sauerkraut. Serves 6.

Quick Roasted Duck

Ingredients

A young, tender wild Duck may be prepared in this manner.

Directions

Place cleaned Duck on rack in a shallow pan. Top with bacon slices and roast in a 400-425 degrees F. oven for 35-45 minutes. Baste with juices and Port wine occasionally while cooking. Season with salt and pepper.

Duck a l'Orange

Ingredients

One Duck
1/4 cup flour
1 to 1 1/2 tsp. salt
2 tbsp. sugar
1 cup hot water
2 tbsp. orange marmalade
1 can (16 oz.) frozen orange juice concentrate, thawed

Directions

Preheat oven to 375 degrees F.

Prick bird skin with a fork around the lower half. Combine all ingredients except waterfowl and pour into the cavity of the Duck. Place in a 2 inch deep roasting pan.

Cook Duck at 350 degrees F. 2 hours or until or until it tests tender.

Baste frequently. Pour drippings in bowl and skim off excess fat, gravy is ready to serve with fowl.

Duck Breasts

Ingredients

2 breasts of Duck
1 pkg. dry onion soup mix
1 apple, sliced
2 cups water
2 tbsp. frozen orange juice (undiluted)

Directions

Fillet breasts. Place breasts on platter and cover with apple and frozen orange juice. Cover with plastic wrap and refrigerate overnight. Place apple, and orange and fillets in 1 1/2 quart oblong baking dish. Empty onion soup and water into dish and bake at 300 degrees for 2 hours. Serve with pan drippings. Serves 4.

Barbecued Duck

Ingredients

1 large Duck
4 tsp. lemon juice
One half cup of your favorite barbecue sauce.
1 tsp. each of salt and chili powder

Directions

Quarter Duck and Sprinkle on salt and chili powder. Brown under broiler, basting frequently with barbecue sauce before serving.

Duck with Orange Slices

Ingredients

Two Duck Breasts
4 orange slices, peeled and seeded
4 slices bacon
1/4 cup butter, melted
1 orange peel, grated
2 tbsp. Frozen orange juice
1 tsp. Frozen lemonade juice
Salt
Pepper

Directions

Sprinkle Duck inside and out with salt and pepper. Cover breast of each bird with an orange and bacon slices, and fasten with string. Place Duck breast-side up in a baking pan and roast at 350 degrees F. for 15-20 minutes or until tender. Baste frequently with combined butter, orange peel, orange juice, and lemon juice. Remove string and sprinkle birds with parsley. Serve with rice or pasts, roasted acorn and/or butternut squash.

Italian Duck

4 Duck Breasts

Fillet Duck breasts from breastbone. Then stand breasts on edge and slice thin.

Marinat for two hours in Italian Salad Dressing. Wrap in bacon and smother with parmesan cheese. Skewer bacon with heavy toothpicks. Broil or grill until bacon is cooked.

Roast Duck

Ingredients

1 Wild Duck
Salt and pepper
1 cup Chopped onions
1 cup Chopped celery
6 Apple slices
6 Thin bacon slices
1 cup Port red wine
Flour for gravy

Directions

Allow one pound of Duck per person. Dry them thoroughly inside and out and rub inside with salt. Fill the insides with onions, apple and celery. Place in an uncovered roasting pan, cover breasts with bacon and cook in a 325 degree oven for 14 minutes per pound. Baste frequently with drippings.

Deglaze pan with wine. Pour off fat and thicken with corn starch for a lighter gravy.

Duck with Mushrooms

Ingredients

1 Duck
1 onion, sliced
1/2 cup of bacon fat or oil
Salt and pepper
2 cups fresh mushrooms—sliced
2-3 sliced onions
2 cups water
1 bay leaf
1 tbsp. sugar
1/8 teaspoon powdered thyme

Directions

Wash and quarter Duck. Saute with onion in bacon fat. Add salt, pepper, water, sugar and bay leaf. Add water, cover and cook 1 1/2 hours over low heat.

Saute mushrooms, onions and salt together. Add to Duck pan and continue to cook 30 more minutes.

Serve with rice.

Duck in Grapes

Ingredients

1 Duck cut up
One quart Stock
6 baby carrots
2 stalks celery
1 medium onion
1 half Pint heavy Cream
2 tsp. Sugar
Salt and pepper
1 apple, cut into wedges
1 bunch of grapes
2 ounces brandy

Directions

Thoroughly wash and clean Duck. Cook Duck pieces in stock with carrots, onions and celery and salt and pepper until tender. Remove from pot. Save stock. Place Duck pieces in a pan or serving dish with cream, and grapes. Simmer briefly. Add brandy and serve.

Duck with Wild Rice

Ingredients

1 dressed Duck salt and pepper water
1 box wild rice mix, cooked

Directions

Put Duck in crock pot. Add salt, pepper, and a small amount of water. Cook on low for 8 hours. Discard skin and bones. Pull meat apart into small pieces. Mix rice and Duck meat. Put in greased casserole dish. Heat thoroughly at 350 degrees. Serve with French or Italian bread.

Duck Stew

Ingredients

A dressed Duck, cut into serving pieces
2 tsp. Garlic powder
1-2 pints water
1/8 cup olive oil
12 baby carrots
1 tsp. Salt
1 tsp. chili powder
4 large onions, chopped
1 green pepper, chopped
3 sliced apples
1 1/2 cups Port wine

Directions

Season Duck with salt, black pepper, and red pepper. Sauté Duck in a large pot. Remove from pot. Saute apples, onions, garlic, celery, and green pepper in same pan.

Replace Duck in pot. Add all other ingredients. Cook over medium heat for 15 minutes, stirring frequently. Add wine. Cover and simmer slowly for 2 1/2 hours or until tender. Replenish water if necessary. Serve over rice.

Marmelade Duck

Ingredients

1 Duck
1 half pkg. small carrots
3 celery stalks
1 medium onion
1 1/2 tsp. salt
1 tsp. Garlic powder
2 cup hot water
6 tbsp. apricot marmalade
One half can (16 oz.) frozen orange juice concentrate, thawed
4 ounces of Sherry

Directions

Preheat oven to 350 degrees F.

Combine all ingredients except Duck and pour into a large roasting pot. Prick Duck skin with a fork to release fat. Add your Duck to the pot.

Cook Duck at 350 degrees F. for 2 hours or until it tests tender. Add water or stock if necessary.

Remove Duck and keep warm. Pour the drippings into a bowl. Remove fat and return drippings to the pot

Remove vegetables and blend on high, then return to pot. Add Sherry, correct seasonings, stir into a gravy bowl and serve with Duck.

Duck Fingers

Ingredients

2 Duck breasts
2 cups buttermilk
2 onions
11/2 box sliced mushrooms1/4 cup oil
1 cup flour salt and pepper
2 tsps. sugar

Directions

Cut meat from breasts into 1/4 inch thick slices and soak them in buttermilk for 6-8 hours. Sauté onions, sugar and mushrooms in olive oil. Clean the milk from the Duck. roll Duck strips in flour and sauté.

Season to taste and serve with sautéd onions and mushrooms

Bavarian Duck

One Duck
1 cup red wine
Salt and pepper to taste
1/2 cup flour
1/4 cup bacon fat
1 cup favorite barbecue sauce
Water

Skin the Duck and cut into serving-size pieces. Cover the pieces with water and wine. Let stand in liquid for 2 to 3 hours or overnight. Drain the Duck pieces and dry them. Salt and pepper each piece and roll it in flour.

Brown the pieces in a skillet in hot fat and put them in a baking dish.

Bavarian Sauce
1/4 cup all-purpose flour
1 cup cooking sherry
1 cup cream
30 Grapes
3 ounces brandy

After Duck has baked, remove and pour off fat. Deglaze the pan drippings into saucepan with the sherry. Bring to a boil, reduce heat to medium, add flour and blend, stirring. Add grapes: fold in brandy and cream.

Remove from stove. Split Duck in half; place into baking pan. cover with sauce, baste and heat 5 minutes. Serves 4.

Duck Breasts with Mushrooms and Heavy Cream

Ingredients

4 boned Duck breasts
1 lb. fresh mushrooms, sliced
I medium onion
2 oz. parmesan cheese
1 cup heavy cream
1/2 teaspoon salt
2 tbsp. Olive oil
1 cup chicken broth
1/2 lemon

Directions

Coat Duck breasts in egg and salt for 1 hour. Lightly sauté the breasts and place in a baking dish.

Sauté mushrooms and onion in your cooking pot. Add all other ingredients except the Duck and the heavy cream. Heat for 10 minutes.

Add Duck breasts and simmer until breasts are pink. Add cream and stir. DO NOT OVERCOOK.

Baked Duck and Barbecue Sauce

Ingredients

One Duck
1 cup red wine
Salt and pepper to taste
1/2 cup flour
1/4 cup bacon fat
1 cup favorite barbecue sauce
Water

Directions

Skin the Duck and cut into serving-size pieces. Cover the pieces with water and wine. Let stand in liquid for 2 to 3 hours or overnight. Drain the Duck pieces and dry them. Salt and pepper each piece and roll it in flour.

Brown the pieces in a skillet in fat and put them in a baking dish. Cover with your favorite Barbecue sauce and add sufficient water.

Correct seasonings add water where necessary and simmer until done.

Pilau of Duck

Ingredients

2 cups roasted Duck meat
1 onion, chopped
Celery leaves to taste
2/3 cup uncooked rice
2 tbsp. butter
3/4 cup finely chopped celery
1 cup leftover Duck gravy

Directions

Cook rice in the liquid until tender (about 1/2 hour).

Next, melt 2 tbsp. butter, add celery and 1 tsp. Onion and sauté covered for 5 minutes. Mix the Duck meat, rice, and 1 cup Duck liquor (or leftover Duck gravy). Serve hot with blended stewed plums or apricots.

Apricot Duck

Ingredients

One large Duck washed and quartered
2 cups fresh apricot preserves
1/4 cup Sherry
1 cup cream
1 tbsp. sugar

Directions

Wash bird. Then marinate Duck in buttermilk to tenderize the meat and get rid of the strong flavor. Wash off buttermilk.

Stuff Duck with apple, orange and celery, and onion. Cook the bird at 350 degrees F.

Be sure to baste often with a mixture of butter and wine or butter and broth. The time required will depend on the size of the bird and the desired amount of doneness. Roast Duck at 350 degrees F.

Mix cream and apricots in saucepan. Add sugar and heat to thicken.

Remove from heat and add sherry. Serves 4.

Duck Breast with Peaches

Ingredients

6 breasts of Duck, boned
2 tbsp. Bacon fat
3 Medium mushrooms
3 Pureed fresh peache
2 Duck livers
1/2 tsp. garlic powder
1 cup chicken stock
1 tbsp. honey
1/2 jar Peach Jam

Directions

Saute mushrooms in bacon fat and set aside.

Brown livers and the breasts on both sides and remove from pan.

Add all other ingredients (honey, stock, peach jam and garlic, etc.) to the pot.

Stir over moderate heat until mixture simmers. Place breasts in pot and warm over low heat about 15 minutes or until done.

Check moisture and seasonings every 5 minutes. Makes 6 servings.

ELK RECIPES

Elk Roast in Foil

Three to four lb. roast
1/2 pkg. of dry onion soup

Preheat oven to 425 degrees. Place roast on piece of heavy duty aluminum foil. Sprinkle 1/2 pkg of dry onion soup over meat. Bring edges of foil together and seal tightly. Place in shallow roasting pan and bake at 350 F for 2 to 2 1/2 hours or until tender. There will be ample juice collected inside foil which can be thickened for gravy.

Elk Steaks

The Elk should hang for 2 or 3 weeks at 35-40 degrees F. and then be properly cut by your butcher. Before cooking, marinate overnight in buttermilk in the frig. Then wash and season before you cook. Buttermilk has an enzyme that breaks down meat fibers and cleans the taste.

To cook young steaks or chops, gentley saute the meat, turning it frequently avoid overcooking. If you like, deglaze the pan with Port Wine and pour sauce over the meat just before serving.

Steaks and chops from young Elk may be cooked in the same manner as beef steaks or lamb chops: broiled, grilled or sauteed.

When broiling, frying or cooking on an outdoor grill, cook quickly and DO NOT OVERCOOK! Game will become tough or dry unless eaten rare. Add Salt & pepper. Garlic and onion powder to taste.

To saute young chops or steaks, heat oil or bacon fat in a skillet. Add meat to the hot skillet and saute it by turning it often on both sides so that it does not overcook and become tough. Salt and pepper to taste.

Elk Pot Roast

4 lbs. Elk Roast
2 cups Port Wine
1 bag baby carrots
6 rough chopped celery stalks
1 can Italian Style tomatoes
Mushrooms
2 tsp. Rosemary
Salt and pepper (or Chili Powder) to taste
2 tsp. Garlic Powder
6 medium Potatoes
2 cups meat stock (any kind)
2 tsp. MSG
3 cups Port wine

Directions

Microwave Potatoes, 2 at a time until tender.

Put all other ingredients in pot and simmer until Elk is tender. Add water as needed. Check seasonings.

Remove Elk roast, blend Vegetables on high to thicken sauce.

Elk Jambalaya

This is a different version of Jambalaya. It is very delicious and easy to make becauce there is almost no cooking.
2 lbs. Elk Tenderloin cut into bite size pieces
1 package zatarain's jambalaya mix
2 1/2 cups water
1/2 cup celery, diced
1/4 cup bamboo shoots
1/4 cup water chestnuts, sliced
1/2 cup bean sprouts
1/2 cup snow peas
1/4 cup white onions, diced
1/3 cup carrots, shredded
1 cup cabbage, shredded
1/4 teaspoon black pepper
3 tbsp. soy sauce
3 tbsp. oil
1 can Italian style tomatoes
1/4 cup cashews

Directions

Cook Zatarain's Jambalaya Mix according to package instructions, omitting the meat.
Reserve.
Heat oil in a wok.
Add all the vegetables and lightly stir fry leaving vegetables crisp.
Add the tomatoes.
Add Elk tidbits. Do not overcook.
Add soy sauce, pepper, and cashews and mix well.
Add cooked Jambalaya, stir to mix well and servee with rice.

Elk Swiss Steaks

Elk round steak sliced thinly
Flour
Salt, and pepper
Onions sliced thin
Mushroom, Soup
1 cup Port wine
1 tsp. Mixed seasonings
1 tsp. MSG

Directions

Mix MSG and seasonings. Sprinkle on steaks.

Gentley saute Elk in Bacon fat. Deglaze pan with Port wine. Add wine sauce to soup.

Mix soup and water to make a sauce. Add enough water to cover steak.

At this point, add soup. Simmer 1-1/2 hours or until tender. Add water if needed during cooking.

Elk Barbecued

20 Elk chops
6 oz Beer
1 lg Onion, chopped
4 tbsp. Bacon fat
2 tbsp. Garlic powder
Sale and Pepper to taste

Marinate Chops in buttermilk and tenderizer overnight. The wash off milk.

Place aluminum foil on hot grill with sides folded up, so there is no runoff of juices. Place chops on foil. Add beer, chopped onion and bacon fat.

Mix garlic powder, pepper and salt and sprinkle mix chops each time you turn them. When chops are done, remove foil from grill.

Elk Ribs Barbecued

Red Wine sufficient to cove ribs in a marinade
1 1/2 c Water
1 cup Currant or plum jelly or jam
1/2 Brown sugar
1/4 medium Onions, finely diced
1/8 tsp. cloves
1/2 tsp. dry mustard
1/2 tsp. garlic powder
1/2 tsp. Salt
6 lb. Elk ribs with some loin meat attached
Freshly ground black pepper to taste

Marinate Elk in buttermilk and tenderizer for one day. The wash off milk.

Preheat oven to 325 degrees. Combine all ingredients except the ribs in a large bowl. Blend well.

Sprinkle ribs with pepper and additional salt. Place in 5 qt. roasting pan in double layer. Roast 1 hour. Pour sauce over ribs. Increase heat to 350 degrees and bake until ribs just begin to char on top, about 1 1/2 hours.

Turn ribs over cover pan and bake about 30 minutes longer, until ribs are tender and sauce is thick. To serve, place ribs on serving platter. Pour sauce over ribs. Makes about 6 servings.

Elk Shoulder

5 lb. shoulder of Elk
1 tsp. garlic powder
2 tbsp. Bacon Fat
4 stalks Celery
15 Baby Carrots
1 big chopped Onion
1 pint Port wine
1 tbsp. sugar
Salt and pepper to taste
1 tsp. MSG
4 cups of noodles

Directions

Pot roast Elk in bacon fat, wine, carrots, garlic and onions until the meat falls off the bone. Add water if necessary.

Remove shoulder. Allow to cool and take meat off bones. Puree vegetablers and sauce in a blender. Correct seasonings. Put cooked noodles on a serving platter. Top with meat. Top the Meat with sauce. Top the sauce with a large strawberry or similar decoration and serve.

Elk Hash

3 cups of ground Elk leftovers.
2 tbsp. Bacon drippings
1 large Chopped Onion
1/2 tsp. Salt
6 small potatoes
1 tbsp. Flour
1 tsp. Garlic powder
3 cups Beef broth
1 tsp.mixed seasonings
1 tbsp.Chili powder

Brown onion and potatoes in bacon fat. Add flour and make a roux:, add Elk, broth and other ingredients. Let simmer until tender.

Elk Jerky

4 lb. Elk roast
1/4 cup salt
1/4 cup brown sugar
2 cups cider
1 cup apple cider
1/4 cup soy sauce
1/4 cup whiskey
2 tsp. Garlic powder
1 tbsp. Chili powder
2 tbsp. Worcestershire sauce

Cut roast into slices 1/4 inch thick by 1 to 2 inches wide. Place meat in marinade, made by combining above ingredients in glass or ceramic bowl. Marinate for at least 24 to 36 hours in a cool place. Remove to wire rack and allow to air dry until glazed. (about 45 minutes). Use hickory chips soaked in water and added to coals to smoke the jerky 12 to 16 hours at 150 to 175 degrees.

Elk Casserole

2 lb. Ground Elk, beef
8-10 slices of bacon
2 cans of tomato soup (un-diluted)
2 cans of whole kernel corn
1 Med. Onion (chopped)
1 Tsp. Garlic Powder
1 pkg. Chili seasoning
2 boxes of Jiffy cornbread mix

In a large skillet cook bacon, remove bacon and drain on paper towel, save drippings. Brown hamburger and onions in drippings. Add the 2 cans of tomato soup, and chili seasoning.

Bake @ 350 degree oven until corn bread mix is golden brown.

Elk Ragu

1 backstrap
1 med. onion
3 med. potatoes
10 Baby Carrots
2 cans cream of mushroom soup
1 crock pot
2 cups red wine

Slice backstrap into chunks. Chop onion and potatoes. Add two cans of cream of mushroom soup plus two cans of water and add all ingredients to crock pot, mix, turn on medium and cook for eight hours. Stir occasionally

Elk Roll ups

Backstrap or other tender Elk cut, cut into strips about 2-3" wide and 4" long
Bacon
Italian dressing
Fresh pablano peppers cut into thin strips
Jack cheese cut into 1/2" x 1/2" slices
Toothpicks

Pound back strap strips to about 1/4" thick. Marinate back strap over night in Italian salad dressing. Lay out one strip of bacon. Place one back strap strip on bacon. Place one pepper strip on back strap.

Place cheese inside pepper strip. Roll tightly and secure with toothpick. Cool over coals until bacon is done.

Elk Backstrap

1 Backstrap/2 Tenderloin
1/2 Cup Red Wine
1/2 Cup Water
1 Onion
1 Bell Pepper
16 oz. Mushrooms
Flour
1 Cup Butter (about)
1 to 1 1/2 cups uncooked rice

Start rice when you begin cooking, everything should be ready at the same time. Marinate meat in your favoritemarinade for 4 to 24 hours. Cut meat into 1/2 inch cubes, flour, heat on low with butter in a large skillet or large pot (needs to be large enough for all contents), and set aside.

Cut up all vegetables. Add them to the wine, water, and meat.

Cook until it starts to thicken (Note: add a little cornstarch mix with COLD water to help thicken if needed). Serve over rice, serves 2 to 4 people

Elk Tid Bits

2 Elk backstraps
4 tbsp.bacon fat
1 can pitted plums
6 Prunes
2 tbsp. garlic power
Salt & Pepper to taste

Heat the bacon drippings in a deep fryer until hot. Combine all dry ingredients in a brown paper bag and shake well to mix. Cut backstraps into fork size chunks. Saute Elk until it is barely pink.

Blend plums and prunes into a sauce and heat in microwave Serve Elk Tid Bits on a platter covered with prune sauce.

Elk Picante

2-3 lbs. of Elk or beef with fat trimmed away
1 1/2 cups Sherry wine
Marinade
1/2 cup Soy Sauce
1/2 cup Worchestershire Sauce
1 oz. Smoke flavoring
1 tbsp. garlic powder
1 tbsp.Chili Powder
1 large mixing bowl

Directions

Set oven to 170 F.

Prepare marinade mixture: Add Soy Sauce, Worcestershire Sauce, smoke flavoring, ground garlic to a large mixing bowl and stir. Cut meat into strips about 1/4 inch thick. Remove as much of the strong tastin fat as possible. Place strips in the marinade and stir. Cover bowl and store in the refrigerator for 24 hr.

Layer the meat strips between two thick layers of paper towels and press to remove excess marinade. You might have to repeat this again with another batch of paper towels. Put in a 170 F until strips are thoroughly dry, usually 3-4 hours.

Smothered Elk

3 lbs. Elk slices
3 mediums onion
3 stalks diced celery
2 tbsp. bacon fat
1/2 cup Sherry or Red Wine
1 pack Peppercorn Gravy Mix
Salt & Pepper
Garlic to taste

Melt the bacon fat in a large pot. Season meat with salt, pepper and Garlic pepper and anything else you like to season your meat with. Mix Peppercorn Gravy Mix with flour. Then flour meat and cook until lightly brown (don't overcook). Set aside sauted meat.

Saute chopped onion in the fat left in the pan. It is now time to turn heat down to low and add wine, salt and pepper to taste. Place all meat back in the pan and place covered in oven on 250 degrees with peppercorn gravy mix. Take a break and come back in 30 or an hour.

Loosen your belt and say the blessing.

Elk Meat Loaf

1 lb. Ground Elk
1 cup Oat meal
1 egg
1/2 Med. Onion chopped
1/2 Med. Sweet pepper chopped
1 Tbsp. Oregano
1 Tbsp. Garlic Powder
1 tsp. Salt
1/2 tsp.Rosemary
2 cups good spaghetti sauce

Combine all ingredients in Mix well. Press into 9x9x2 loaf pan. Cook in 350 degree oven for 25 to 30 minutes. Cover with Spaghetti Sauce. Great served with Mashed potato's.

Elk Steak

5 Elk steaks cut 1-inch thick—backstrap & tenderloin are the best
2 eggs
3/4 cup buttermilk
1 cup all-purpose flour salt & pepper seasoned salt
1/4 cup canola oil
1/2 cup sherry

Beat eggs and mix with buttermilk. Set aside. Mix all-purpose flour, salt, pepper, and seasoned salt. Dip steaks into buttermilk/egg mixture and then dredge them on both sides in the flour mixture. Fry for 7-10 minutes on medium-high heat until golden brown or desired doneness.
Add sherry and deglaze the pan.

Elk in a Wok

One large Chinese Wok skillet
2 cups small strips of Elk
2 tbsp. canola or olive oil
1 large clove garlic, crushed
1 cup chopped green peppers
2 cups sliced mushrooms
1 cup diced onion
1 cup cubed potatoes
1 cup corn kernels (frozen work well)
1/3 cup worchestershire sauce
1/3 cup Port Wine salt & pepper oregano leaves

Heat oil in wok until very hot. Add crushed garlic clove and let sizzle a minute or so. Add Elk strips and saute for a few minutes. Add potatoes and onions next and saute for about 5 minutes, stirring every so often.

Add worchestershire sauce and red wine vinegar. Add salt, pepper and oregano leaves as needed to taste. Lastly, add green peppers, mushrooms and corn kernels, and cook only long enough that vegetables don't go limp. Tastes great with a topping of freshly grated parmesan cheese.

Elk Crown Roast

1 or 2 whole Elk rib sections with backstraps attached
1 tsp. garlic powder
1 tsp. salt
1 tsp. black pepper
3 lb. Elk and Bacon Burger
1 can (20 oz.) apple slices with juice, chopped
10 slices dried bread; cut into 1/2 inch cubes
2 Tbsp. raisins
3/4 tsp. salt
1 tsp. cinnamon
1/2 tsp. cardamom
1/4 tsp. allspice
Apple-Orange Cranberry Liqueur Sauce

Note: The assembly of the crown is difficult. It is recommended that you take two whole rib sections, with backstraps still attached, to a butcher and have them to assemble the crown roast.

Mix garlic salt and pepper together; rub mixture into all sides of roast. Place seasoned roast, bone ends up, in a shallow roasting pan. Add Apples, Raisins, cinnamon, bread and allspice to Burger/Sausage and saute in a skillet until brown. Drain excess liquids. Fill center of crown roast with sausage mixture; cover with aluminum foil.

Insert meat thermometer into center of roast. Bake at 325 degrees until meat thermometer reads 135 degrees to 140 degrees. (Time varies according to size and age of animal.) Add decorative frills for the top of each crown point, (available a local butcher shop.) Serve with Apple-Orange Cranberry Liqueur Sauce. Serves 10 to 14.

Stuffed Elk Chops

6 Elk chops, cut 1 1/2" thick
1 1/2 cups garlic croutons
1/2 cup apple, chopped
1/2 cup Cheddar cheese, shredded
2 tbsp. raisins
2 tbsp. Bacon Fat
2 tbsp. orange juice
1/4 tsp. salt
1/8 tsp. cinnamon
Apple-Orange Cranberry Liqueur Sauce

Preheat oven to 350 degrees. Cut a pocket in the side of each Elk chop. Mix together the croutons, apple, cheese and currants. In another bowl, combine melted Butter, orange juice, salt and cinnamon. Pour butter mixture over the crouton mixture and mix gently. Lightly stuff the Elk chops with the butter-crouton mixture.

Place the stuffed chops in a shallow baking pan and bake uncovered for 1 hour. Cover with aluminum foil and bake for another 15 minutes. Serve with Apple-Orange Cranberry Liqueur Sauce. Serves 6.

Elk Tenderloin

1 Elk tenderloin
1 Pint Buttermilk
1 Pint meat stock
1/2 tsp. ground thyme
1 tsp. black pepper
Berry Jam/Jelly
parsley sprigs
yellow squash slices

Clean and wash tenderloin: then mairinate in buttermilk. 3-4 hours or overnight

Mix thyme, pepper, salt, garlic and sugar with Berry Jam/Jelly for sauce

Roast tenderloin to 140 F. Cook only until rare because Elk, moose and venison have very little fat. The meat should be slightly pink to red in the center and quite moist.

Serve on a platter with Berry Sauce. Decorate with parsley sprigs and yellow squash slices. Serves 4 to 6.

Elk Stir Fry

1 lb. Elk steak
2 tbsp. olive oil
8 baby carrots
1/2 cup celery
1 part broccoli
1/2 cup salted peanuts
1 tsp. Garlic Powder
1/2 cup soy sauce
1/2 tsp. crushed red pepper
1 teaspoon cumin
Cooked noodles—excluding seasoning packet

Slice steaks cross grain and marinade in soy sauce for one day. Throw a little oil in a hot wok to avoid sticking. Stir in Elk for about 1 minute. Add other ingredients, including seasoning, stirring frequently. Add additional soy sauce to coat all ingredients. Stir in noodles and serve immediately.

Elk Stew

1/2 lb. Bacon or salt pork
2 lb. Elk steak
1/2 lb. Bacon or salt pork
2 tbsp. flour
6 cups of stock
1 can stewed tomatoes or preferably zucchini
8 small carrots carrots
2 Stalks celery diced
2 tbsp. sugar
7 small onions garlic to taste
1 cup peas
Salt and pepper to taste

Cut bacon into 1" cubes and saute in large saucepan until lightly browned.

Remove and set aside. Cut Elk into 1 1/2 or 2" pieces and brown over high heat in bacon fat. Stir in flour and make a roux. Lower heat and let brown 2-3 minutes. Then add stock and stir till smooth. Simmer 1 hour or more until Elk begins to get tender, add more liquid as necessary.

Add all the other ingredients, except peas, and continue to simmer to make a thick stew. Simmer peas in a separate pan until done. Strain and spoon over or around stew when served. Serve with corn muffins, potatoes or parsnips and a salad.

Elk Hamburgers

Young Elk Ground up is a rich tasting delicious treat. You should add fat, preferably Bacon Fat to all Elk Hamburgers

Elk Hamburger

5 lbs. lean Elk
2 tbsp. sage
1-1 1/2 cups bacon fat
1 tbsp. salt
1 tbsp. liquid smoke
5 tbsp. sugar
2 tbsp. pepper

Grind and thoroughly mix all ingredients, form into patties and pan fry. Wrap individually in butter fat and it will keeps for 1 year in the freezer.

German Style Elk Hamburger

2 lbs. Ground Elk
1 Knockwurst, skinned and diced
Salt and pepper
4 ounces Bacon fat
1 small onion
1 tsp. Dill garlic powder to taste
3 ounces of Beer

Mix sausage and ground Elk. Combine with remaining ingredients. Brown until almost done. Add beer to deglaze the pan and make a sauce.

Polish Style Elk Hamburger

2 lbs. Ground Elk
1/2 Kielb.asa, skinned and diced
Salt and pepper
4 ounces Bacon fat
1 small onion
1 tsp. Dill garlic powder to taste
3 ounces of Beer

Mix sausage and ground Elk. Combine with remaining ingredients. Brown until almost done. Add beer to deglaze the pan and make a sauce.

French Style Elk Hamburger

2 lbs. Ground Elk
1/4 lb. Brie Cheese
Salt and pepper
4 ounces Bacon fat
1 small onion
1 tsp. Thyme garlic powder to taste
3 ounces of Red Wine

Combine all ingredients. Brown until rare. Add beer to deglaze the pan and make a sauce

Italian Style Elk Hamburger

2 lbs. Ground Elk
1/4 lb. Gorgonzola Cheese
Salt and pepper
4 ounces Bacon fat
1 small onion
1 tsp. Oregano garlic powder to taste
3 ounces of Red Wine

Combine all ingredients. Brown until rare. Add beer to deglaze the pan and make a sauce

Danish Style Elk Hamburger

2 lbs. Ground Elk
1/4 lb. Danish Blue Cheese
Salt and pepper
4 ounces Bacon fat
1 small onion
1 tsp. Thyme garlic powder to taste
3 ounces of Beer

Combine all ingredients. Brown until rare. Add beer to deglaze the pan and make a sauce

Irish Style Elk Hamburger

2 lbs. Ground Elk
1/4 lb. Cheddar Cheese
Salt and pepper
4 ounces Bacon fat
1 small onion
1 tsp. Thyme garlic powder to taste
3 ounces of Stout

Combine all ingredients. Brown until rare. Add beer to deglaze the pan and make a sauce

English Style Elk Hamburger

2 lbs. Ground Elk
1/4 lb. Cheddar Cheese
Salt and pepper
4 ounces Bacon fat
1 small onion
1 tsp. Thyme garlic powder to taste
3 ounces of Scotch Whiskey

Combine all ingredients. Brown until rare. Add beer to deglaze the pan and make a sauce

Mexican Style Elk Hamburger

2 lbs. Ground Elk
1/4 lb. Jalapeno Pepper Cheese
1 tbsp.Salt
4 ounces Bacon fat
1 small onion
1 tbsp. Chili Powder garlic powder to taste
3 ounces of Corona Beer

Combine all ingredients. Brown until rare. Add beer to deglaze the pan and make a sauce

American Style Elk Hamburger

2 lbs. Ground Elk
1/4 lb. Monterey Jack Cheese
Salt and pepper
4 ounces Bacon fat
1 small onion
1 tsp. Chili Powder garlic powder to taste
3 ounces of Bourbon Whiskey

Combine all ingredients. Brown until rare. Add beer to deglaze the pan and make a sauce

FROG RECIPES

Crunchy Frog Legs

5 lbs. small frog legs
1/4 of a cup lemon juice
Crushed ice
1 cup milk
6 eggs, separated
2 tbsp. olive oil
1 tsp. Sugar
1/4 tsp. salt
Salt and pepper
1 1/2 cups all-purpose flour
Vegetable oil

Wash frog legs thoroughly. Place in a large Dutch oven; sprinkle with lemon juice, and cover with crushed ice. Refrigerate 1 to 3 hours.

Combine milk, egg yols, olive oil, sugar and 1/4 tsp. salt; mix well. Beat egg whites until stiff; fold into batter.

Sprinkle frog legs with salt and pepper; dip each in batter, and dredge in flour. Fry until golden brown in deep oil heated to 375 degrees F. Drain on paper towels.

Yield: about 6 servings.

Frog Legs in Cream Sauce

Six frog legs salt
Pepper
Flour
Cooking Oil
30 grapes
2 cans of mushroom soup
1 cup heavy cream
2 ounces Brandy
1 tsp. sugar

Preheat oven to 350 degrees F. Sprinkle seasoned salt and pepper on Frog Legs. Parboil for 15 minutes. Then put in a greased baking dish and set aside. Combine the 2 cans of soup in a saucepan with the heavy cream and heat. Add the grapes. Pour soup mixture over the frogs' legs, add your grapes and bake 1 hour. Mix in brandy before serving. Also good with pheasant and quail.

Frog Legs Forestiere

Six pairs of Frog Legs
1 quart chicken or turkey stock
1 onion
2 celery stalks
12 baby carrots
3 cloves mashed garlic salt
1 sp. sgar pepper
1/2 can Stewed tomatoes

Directions

Wash frog legs thoroughly. Pit in oven proof serving dish. Add stock and tomatoes. Thin slice 1 onion and chop celery into small pieces. Add to pot with water to cover.

Bake at low simmer untill tender. Check salt-sugar balance. Let sit for two hours. Warm and serve

GOOSE RECIPES

About Roasting Goose

Wash bird well. Then marinate in buttermilk to tenderize the meat and get rid of the strong flavor. Stuff goose with apple, orange, celery, and onion. You may cook the birds slowly at 350 degrees F or quickly at 450 degrees F. Be sure to baste often with a mixture of butter and wine or butter and broth. The time required will depend on the size of the bird and the desired amount of doneness. Geese will require 20-30 minutes at 450 degrees F. and 1 to 1 1/2 hours at 350 degrees F. A goose will take 15-30 minutes longer than a Duck.

As a general rule, the bird is done when the leg can be moved back and forth easily. Wild goose and geese have less fat than domestic varieties and do not create as much mess in the oven.

Goose or Duck can also be cooked in a bag with seasonings. At 350 degrees F, Duck will take about 1 1/2 hours. Plan on 2 hours cooking time for a goose in a bag.

A large Duck will feed 2 people, a smaller Duck or a teal will feed 1 person. A 6 lb. dressed goose will feed 4 to 6 people.

Stewed Goose

Ingredients

1 goose or 2 Ducks, cut up
I can zucchini in tomato sauce
Salt and pepper
2 apple, cut into wedges
15 baby carrots
5 small potatoes
2 Cut up celery stalks
2 tbsp. Bacon drippings
1 tbsp. sugar
Water
1 cup Port Wine

Combine all ingredients in a pot. Cover with wine and water and cook until tender. Discard apple.

Baked Goose

Ingredients

1 Canada Goose
Salt, pepper
1 tbsp. Sugar
1 tbsp. cinnamon
1 tbsp. ginger
1 cup Italian Salad derssing
3/4 cup cooking sherry

Directions

Thoroughly wash and rinse goose

Sprinkle salt, pepper, sugar, ginger and cinnamon over entire goose. Rub into skin. Combine sherry and pour over goose. Bake for 1 hour 350 degrees with top on roasting pan. Take top off; broil 8 minutes. Turn goose breast side up and broil 8 minutes.

SAUCE: Deglaze pan with sherry, Pour off oil, add flour to make a wine sauce. Pour over thinly sliced goose.

Stuffed Goose

Ingredients

One wild goose
Giblets from goose
4 cups bread crumbs
2 med. onions
2 apples, diced
1/4 tsp. sage
1/4 tsp. garlic powder
2 tsp. salt
1/2 tsp. pepper
1 tbsp. sugar
1 cup sherry

Directions

Place goose in roasting pan and roast for about 20 minutes per pound of goose at 350 degrees. Baste often.

Cook giblets until tender; reserve liquid. Chop giblets and add to bread crumbs, onions, apples, and seasonings. Add liquid from giblets to moisten stuffing.

Pour off fat. Deglaze pan with sherry. Add some salt and pepper to correct seasonings. This makes 6-8 servings.

Goose with Sauerkraut

Ingredients

1 goose cleaned and washed
1 tbsp. salt
1 tsp. Chili powder
1 tsp. garlic
1 apples, quartered
1 onions, quartered
4 slices of bacon
2 cups water
3 cups canned sauerkraut
1 tsp. caraway seeds
2 tbsp. Brown sugar
4 slices well done bacon

Directions

Preheat oven to 350 F.

Season Geese with mixture of salt, chili powder, and garlic. Quarter apples and onions and stuff half into bird cavities. Cover breasts with uncooked bacon and place into baking pan. Place pan in preheated 350 degrees F. oven; bake 3 hours. Baste every 30 minutes.

Soak sauerkraut in water twice. It is very salty. Then combine sauerkraut, caraway seeds, crumbled bacon and brown sugar in pan. Mix well. Simmer for 1 and a half hours on low, adding water as needed. Place in oven 20 minutes before Geese are done.

Serve quartered goose or Ducks on sauerkraut. Serves 6.

Quick Roasted Goose

Ingredients

A young, tender wild goose may be prepared in this manner.

Directions

Place cleaned goose on rack in a shallow pan. Top with bacon slices and roast in a 400-425 degrees F. oven for 35-45 minutes. Baste with juices and Port wine occasionally while cooking. Season with salt and pepper.

Goose a l'Orange

Ingredients

One goose
1/4 cup flour
1 to 1 1/2 tsp. salt
2 tbsp. sugar
1 cup hot water
2 tbsp. orange marmalade
1 can (16 oz.) frozen orange juice concentrate, thawed

Directions

Preheat oven to 375 degrees F.

Prick bird skin with a fork around the lower half. Combine all ingredients except waterfowl and pour into the cavity of the goose. Place in a 2 inch deep roasting pan.

Cook goose at 350 degrees F. 2 hours or until or until it tests tender. Baste frequently. Pour drippings in bowl and skim off excess fat, gravy is ready to serve with fowl.

Goose Breasts

Ingredients

2 breasts of goose
1 pkg. dry onion soup mix
1 apple, sliced
2 cups water
2 tbsp. frozen orange juice (undiluted)

Directions

Fillet breasts. Place breasts on platter and cover with apple and frozen orange juice. Cover with plastic wrap and refrigerate overnight. Place apple, and orange and fillets in 1 1/2 quart oblong baking dish. Empty onion soup and water into dish and bake at 300 degrees for 2 hours. Serve with pan drippings. Serves 4.

Barbecued Goose

Ingredients

1 large goose
4 tsp. lemon juice
One half cup of your favorite barbecue sauce.
! tsp. each of salt and chili powder

Directions

Quarter goose and Sprinkle on salt and chili powder. Brown under broiler, basting frequently with barbecue sauce before serving.

Goose w Orange Slices

Ingredients

Two Goose Breasts
4 orange slices, peeled and seeded
4 slices bacon
1/4 cup butter, melted
1 orange peel, grated
2 tbsp. orange juice
1 tsp. lemon juice
Parsley, chopped
Salt
Pepper

Directions

Sprinkle Goose inside and out with salt and pepper. Cover breast of each bird with an orange and bacon slice, and fasten with string. Place Goose breast-side up in a baking pan and roast at 350 degrees F. for 15-20 minutes or until tender. Baste frequently with combined butter, orange peel, orange juice, and lemon juice. Remove string and sprinkle birds with parsley. Serve with roasted orange and bacon slices, pureed squash, and baby brussels sprouts.

Italian Goose

Fillet Goose breasts from breastbone. Cut cross-grain into 1/2 in thick steaks. Tendersize Goose steaks with meat hammer. Marinate 2 hours in Italian Salad Dressing. Wrap in bacon and smother with parmesan cheese. Skewer bacon with heavy toothpicks. Broil or grill until bacon is cooked.

Roast Goose

Ingredients

1 Wild Goose
Salt and pepper
1 cup Chopped onions
1 cup Chopped celery
6 Apple slices
6 Thin bacon slices
1 cup Port red wine
Flour for gravy

Directions

Allow one pound of Goose per person. Dry them thoroughly inside and out and rub inside with salt. Fill the insides with onions, apple and celery.

Place in an uncovered roasting pan, cover breasts with bacon and cook in a 325 degree oven for 14 minutes per pound. Baste frequently with drippings to which the dry red wine was added.

Deglaze pan with wine. Pour off fat and thicken with corn starch for a lighter gravy.

Goose with Mushrooms

Ingredients

1 Goose
1 onion, sliced
1/2 cup of bacon fat or oil
Salt and pepper
2 cups fresh mushrooms—sliced
2-3 sliced onions 2 cups water
1 bay leaf
1 tbsp. sugar
1/8 teaspoon powdered thyme

Directions

Wash and quarter Goose. Saute with onion in bacon fat. Add salt, pepper, water, and bay leaf. Cook 1 1/2 hours over low heat.

Saute mushrooms, onions salt and sugar together. Add to Goose and continue to cook 30 more minutes.

Serve with rice.

Goose in Grapes

Ingredients

1 goose cut up
One quart Stock
6 baby carrots
2 stalks celery
1 medium onion
One half Pint heavy Cream
1 tbsp. Sugar
Salt and pepper
1 apple, cut into wedges
1 bunch of grapes
2 ounces brandy

Directions

Thoroughly wash and clean goose. Cook goose pieces in stock with carrots, onions and celery and salt and pepper until tender. Remove from pot.

Save stock. Place goose pieces in a pan or serving dish with cream, and grapes. Simmer briefly. Add brandy and serve.

Goose with Wild Rice

Ingredients

1 dressed Goose salt and pepper water
1 small box wild rice mix, cooked

Directions

Put Goose in crock pot. Add salt, pepper, and a small amount of water.

Cook on low for 8 hours. Discard skin and bones. Pull meat apart into small pieces. Mix rice and Goose meat. Put in greased casserole dish. Heat thoroughly at 350 degrees. Serve with French or Italian bread.

Goose Stew

Ingredients

A dressed Goose, cut into serving pieces
2 tsp. Garlic powder
1-2 pints water
1/8 cup olive oil
12 baby carrots
1 tsp. Salt
1 tsp. chili powder
4 large onions, chopped
1 green pepper, chopped
3 sliced apples
1 1/2 cups Port wine

Directions

Season Goose with salt, black pepper, and red pepper. Sauté Goose in a large pot. Remove from pot. Saute apples, onions, garlic, celery, and green pepper in same pan.

Replace Goose in pot. Add all other ingredients. Cook over medium heat for 15 minutes, stirring frequently. Add wine. Cover and cook slowly for 2 1/2 hours or until tender. Replenish water if necessary. Serve over rice.

Marmelade Goose

Ingredients

1 Goose
1 half pkg. small carrots
3 celery stalks
1 medium onion
1 1/2 tsp. salt
1 tsp. Garlic powder
2 cup hot water
6 tbsp. apricot marmalade
One half can (16 oz.) frozen orange juice concentrate, thawed
4 ounces of Sherry

Directions

Preheat oven to 350 degrees F.

Combine all ingredients except goose and pour into a large roasting pot. Prick goose skin with a fork. Add your goose to the pot.

Cook Goose at 350 degrees F. for 2 hours or until it tests tender. Add water or stock if necessary.

Remove goose and keep warm. Deglaze the pot with Sherry and pour drippings in bowl. Remove fat and return drippings to the pot

Remove vegetables and blend on high, then return to pot. Correct seasonings, stir into a gravy bowl and serve with goose.

Goose Fingers

Ingredients

2 Goose breasts
2 cups buttermilk
2 onions
1/4 cup oil
1 cup flour salt and pepper
2 tsps. sugar

Directions

Cut meat from breasts into 1/4 inch thick slices and soak them in buttermilk for 6-8 hours. Sauté onions sugar and mushrooms in olive oil. Drain milk, roll Goose strips in flour and sauté. Season to taste and serve with sautéed onions and mushrooms

Bavarian Goose

One Goose
1 cup red wine
Salt and pepper to taste
1/2 cup flour
1/4 cup bacon fat
1 cup favorite barbecue sauce
Water

Skin the Goose and cut into serving-size pieces. Cover the pieces with water and wine. Let stand in liquid for 2 to 3 hours or overnight. Drain the Goose pieces and dry them. Salt and pepper each piece and roll it in flour.

Brown the pieces in a skillet in hot fat and put them in a baking dish.

Bavarian Sauce

1/4 cup all-purpose flour
1 cup cooking sherry
1 cup cream
30 Grapes
3 ounces brandy

After Goose has baked, remove and pour off fat. Deglaze the pan drippings into saucepan with the sherry. Bring to a boil, reduce heat to medium, add flour and blend, stirring. Add grapes: fold in brandy and cream. Remove from stove. Split Goose in half; place into baking pan. cover with sauce, baste and heat 5 minutes. Serves 4.

Goose Breasts with Mushrooms and Heavy Cream

Ingredients

4 boned goose breasts
1 lb. fresh mushrooms, sliced
I medium onion
2 oz. parmesan cheese
1 cup heavy cream
1/2 teaspoon salt
2 tbsp. Olive oil
1 cup chicken broth
1/2 lemon

Directions

Coat goose breasts in egg and salt for 1 hour. Lightly sauté the breasts and place in a baking dish.

Sauté mushrooms and onion in your cooking pot. Add all other ingredients except the Goose and the heavy cream. Heat for 10 minutes.

Add goose breasts and heavy cream and simmer until breasts are pink. DO NOT OVERCOOK.

Baked Goose and Barbecue Sauce

Ingredients

One Goose
1 cup red wine
Salt and pepper to taste
1/2 cup flour
1/4 cup bacon fat
1 cup favorite barbecue sauce
Water

Directions

Skin the Goose and cut into serving-size pieces. Cover the pieces with water and wine. Let stand in liquid for 2 to 3 hours or overnight. Drain the Goose pieces and dry them. Salt and pepper each piece and roll it in flour.

Brown the pieces in a skillet in hot fat and put them in a baking dish.

Cover with your favorite Barbecue sauce and add sufficient water.

Correct seasonings add water where necessary and simmer until done.

Pilau of Goose

Ingredients

2 cups roasted Goose meat
1 onion, chopped
Celery leaves to taste
2/3 cup uncooked rice
2 tbsp. butter
3/4 cup finely chopped celery
1 cup leftover Goose gravy

Directions

Cook rice in the liquid until tender (about 1/2 hour).

Next, melt 2 tbsp. butter, add celery and 1 tsp. Onion and sauté covered for 5 minutes. Mix the Goose meat, rice, and 1 cup Goose liquor (or leftover Goose gravy). Serve hot with blended stewed plums or apricots.

Apricot Goose

Ingredients

One large Goose cleaned and washed
2 cups fresh apricot preserves or canned apricots
1/4 cup Sherry
1 cup cream
1 tbsp. sugar

Directions

Wash bird. Then marinate goose in buttermilk to tenderize the meat and get rid of the strong flavor. Stuff goose with apple, orange and celery, and onion. Cook the bird at 350 degrees F.

Be sure to baste often with a mixture of butter and wine or butter and broth. The time required will depend on the size of the bird and the desired amount of doneness. Roast goose at 350 degrees F. for 2 hours.

Drain liquid from apricots into saucepan. Add cream and sugar and heat to thicken. Remove from heat and add apricots and sherry. Serves 4.

Goose Breast with Peaches

Ingredients

3 breasts of Goose, boned
2 tbsp. Bacon fat
3 Medium mushrooms
2 tbsp. Grated orange rind
1/4 cup Orange juice
1 Pureed fresh peache
2 Goose livers
1/2 tsp. garlic powder
1 cup chicken stock
1 tbsp. honey
1/2 jar Peach Jam

Directions

Saute mushrooms in bacon fat and set aside.

Brown livers and the breasts on both sides and remove from pan.

Add all other ingredients (Orange juice, orange rind, honey, stock and garlic, etc.) to the pot.

Stir over moderate heat until mixture simmers. Place breasts in pot and cook over low heat about 20 minutes or until done.

Makes 6 servings.

GROUSE RECIPES

Grouse with Orange Sauce

Four grouse
4 orange slices, peeled and seeded
4 slices bacon
1/4 cup butter, melted
1 cup frozen orange juice
1 tsp. lemon juice
Parsley, chopped
Salt
Pepper

Sprinkle grouse inside and out with salt and pepper. Cover breast of each bird with an orange and bacon slice, and fasten with string. Place grouse breast-side up in a baking pan and roast at 350 degrees F. for 15-20 minutes or until tender.

Baste frequently with combined butter and frozen orange juice. Remove string and sprinkle birds with parsley. Serve with roasted orange and bacon slices, puree of butternut squash and baby brussels sprouts, boiled and then sauted with yogurt.

Grouse Breasts with Cumberland Sauce

Four grouse breasts
One half cup chopped celery
Salt and pepper
1/4 cup butter
6 small onions chopped
2 tbsp. sherry wine
1 tbsp. chopped parsley
Salt
Pepper

Cook Celery and onions in microwave. Rub grouse breasts with salt, and pepper. Saute quickly in butter until very rare. Add sherry, onions and celeryroth.

Cumberland Sauce

1 /1/2 cups of wine
1/3 cup rasins
1 cup current or Blackberry jelly
1/8th tsp. Cloves
2 tbsp. frozen OJ
1 half tsp. Corn starch
2 tbsp. dark brown sugar 1/2 tsp. salt
1 half tsp.ginger

Mix cornstarch in a little heated wine. Combine with th rest of the ingredients and serve warm.
Serve breasts on toast and top with sauce.

Ginger Grouse

1-2 grouse
1/2 cup margarine
1 can beef broth
1/2 can water
2 tbsp. flour
1/4 cup margarine
1 tbsp. soy sauce
Onion
Green pepper
Tomato, cut into chunks
Cooked rice, white or wild
1 tsp. Ginger powder
Salt
Pepper

Clean and skin grouse. Cut meat from breast and slice into 1/4-inch slices. Brown slices in 1/2 cup butter or margarine. Slice a small onion and add to meat in pan.

Heat slowly so butter does not brown or burn. To make sauce, melt margarine in pan, add flour and stir. Add beef broth, water, and soy sauce.

Cook until thickened and season as desired. Slice green pepper and onion thinly and add to gravy. Cook slowly until both are tender crisp. Add meat to gravy and add tomato chunks. Cook gently. Serve over hot rice.

Grouse in Sour Cream

1 grouse, cut into serving pieces
2 tbsp. Bacon Fat
Flour
Salt
Pepper
1 cup sour cream
3 tbsp. dry onion soup mix
1/2 cup milk

Coat bird with flour; salt and pepper to taste. Brown grouse in fat. Combine sour cream, soup mix, and milk; pour over bird. Cover and bake at 350 degrees F. for 1 hour or until tender.

Creamed Grouse

2 grouse, skinned and boned
1 onion, chopped
1 cup celery, chopped
1/4 cup margarine
1/4 cup flour
2 cups water
2 cups heavy cream
3 chicken bouillon cubes
1 tsp. garlic powder
1 tbsp. Ranch style salad dressing
Salt
Pepper

Soak grouse overnight in salt water. Put meat in Dutch oven or pressure cooker. Add onion, celery, and water. Simmer 1 1/2-2 hours until tender or pressure cook 20 minutes at 15 pounds. Remove meat from liquid.

Cool and break meat into small pieces. Melt margarine, blend in flour, stir in milk, and stir constantly until thick. Add bouillon cubes to liquid from meat, heat and dissolve cubes. Add sauce to liquid and meat. Add Ranch dressing and salt and pepper to taste.

Italian Grouse Breasts

Ingredients

4 Grouse breasts
4 tbsp. Bacon Fat
1 cup Italian Salad Dressing
4 slices bacon
2 slices Mozzarella
4 tbsp. Parmesan
1 cup pasta sauce
1 tsp. MSG

Directions

Fillet Grouse breasts from breastbone. Cut cross-grain into 1/2 in thick steaks. Flatten steaks with meat hammer. Marinate 2 hours in Italian Salad Dressing.

Divide Mozzarella cheese in half. Wrap in bacon. Skewer bacon with heavy toothpicks. Broil or grill until bacon is cooked.

Divide Mozzarella cheese in half and top breasts while hot with Mozzarella and then Parmesan cheese. Top with hot pasta sauce and serve.

Grouse in Orange Cream Sauce

1 grouse, cut into serving pieces
1 tbsp. flour
1 tsp. salt
3/4 tsp. sugar
4 tbsp. frozen orange juice
1/4 tsp. allspice
3/4 tsp. garlic
1 tsp. paprika
2 tbsp. bacon fat
4 ounces of sherry

Mix flour, salt, sugar, allspice, garlic, and paprika in a fat bowl or pan. Dip grouse pieces in flour mixture to coat. Brown pieces gently in bacon fat over low heat, add sherry, cover, and simmer until tender add stock if necessary.

MOOSE RECIPES

Mooseburgers

If the moose or venison meat is very lean, add some bacon fat to the meat when having it ground (10-15%).
Mix with onion soup mix (1 packet per pound of meat) for more flavor.
You may cook these burgers the same as any beef-burger—saute, broil, or grill. Be sure not to over-cook as this will dry out your game meat.

Moose Roast

3-4 lb. Roast
1/2 pkg. of dry onion soup

Preheat oven to 425 degrees. Place roast on piece of heavy duty aluminum foil. Sprinkle 1/2 pkg of dry onion soup over meat. Bring edges of foil together and seal tightly. Place in shallow roasting pan and bake for 2 to 2 1/2 hours. There will be ample juice collected inside foil which can be thickened for gravy.

Moose Steaks

Moose should always be marinated in buttermilk overnight. To cook young steaks or chops, heat a heavy skillet until quite hot and add half butter and half oil. Saute the meat, turning it frequently to brown to taste. If you like, flame the meat with cognac just before serving.

Steaks and chops from young animals may be cooked in the same manner as beef steaks or lamb chops: broiled, grilled or sauteed.

When broiling or cooking on an outdoor grill, cook quickly and DO NOT OVERCOOK! Game will become tough or dry with long broiling or frying. Salt & pepper to taste.

To saute young chops or steaks, melt butter in a heavy skillet. Add meat to the hot skillet and saute it by turning it often on both sides so that it will brown without charring. Salt and pepper to taste.

Moose Casserole

2 lbs. of venison or moose meat cubed
1 can mushroom soup
1 pkg dry onion soup mix
1 cup canned tomatoes or 2 fresh tomatoes

Preheat oven to 325 degrees F. Place meat in casserole dish and add mushroom soup, dry onion soup mix, and tomatoes. Cover and bake for 2 hours.

Moose Meat Loaf

1 1/2 lbs. ground venison or moose
1 tsp. minced onion
1 cup milk
1 egg
1 1/2 tsp. salt
1 cup oatmeal

Preheat oven to 350 degrees F. Mix all ingredients together. Place in a greased 9x5x3 inch loaf pan. Bake 1 hour.

Moose Roast in Bag

3-4 lb. roast 4" thick salt and pepper
1 tsp. sugar
1 tsp.accent
1 medium onion quartered
2 bay leaves, crumbled
1/2 cup dry red wine

Preheat oven to 325 degrees. Shake 1 tablespoon flour in small size (10x16") brown-in-bag and place in 2 inch deep roasting pan. Pour wine into bag and stir until flour is well mixed. Rub meat with salt and pepper.

Place meat in bag. Put onion and bay leaves around roast. Close bag with twist tie and make 6 half-inch slits in top. Cook for 2 to 2 1/2 hours.

Moose Casserole

3 lbs. moose meat cut in chunks
One half lb. Sausage (knockwurst or Kielb.ase) in chinks
3 large (6 small) carrots)
2 stalks of Celery diced
I large onion diced
Garlic
Salt and Pepper
One half tsp. oregano
One half tsp. Thyme
One tsp. sugar
One half tsp.Accent
One quarter cup tomato paste

Put moose into pot. Add some bacon fat to the Meat. Saute until brown. Add All other ingredients. add more water if needed. Cook until tender. Remove vegetables and blend. Return gravy to pot. Be sure not to over-cook as this will dry out your game meat. Side dish of boiled and buttered carrots. Side dish of boiled and butgtered onions. Side dish of potatoes.

Directions

Brown moose and sausage in a large pot, add all vegetable and sauté till lightly browned. Add red wine, broth and seasonings. Let simmer 30 minutes. Remove meat. Blend sauce and vegetables from the pot to to thicken. Put thickened sauce back into pot or serving dish and serve

Serves five.

Easy Moose Stew

Cut moose into chunks
Add some bacon fat to the Meat
Place in pot wit water to cover
Add Celery, Onion and Carrots
Add salt, pepper, garlic, oregano sugar and accent

Remove vegetables and blend Be sure not to over-cook as this will dry out your game meat. Side dish of boiled and buttered carrots
Side dish of boiled and butgtered onions.
Side dish of potatoes

Directions

Brown moose and sausage in a large pot, add all vegetable and sauté till lightly browned. Add red wine, broth and seasonings. Let simmer 30 minutes. Remove meat. Blend sauce and vegetables from the pot to to thicken. Put thickened sauce back into pot or serving dish and serve
Serves five.

Moose Hash

3 cups Cooked and ground Moose leftovers
3 tbsp.Bacon fat
1 large Onion, chopped
2 large Diced potatoes
1 tbsp. flour
1 Clove garlic, minced
3 cups Beef broth
1/4 ts Black pepper
1/4 ts salt
1/4 tsp. Thyme
1/2 tbsp. sage

Brown onion and potatoes in bacon fat. Add flour and make a roux:, add Moose, broth and other ingredients. Let simmer until tender.

Barbequed Chops

20 Moose chops
6 oz Beer
1 lg Onion, chopped
4 pats of butter
2 oz Garlic

Place aluminum foil on hot grill with sides folded up, so there is no runoff of juices. Place chops on foil. Add beer, chopped onion and butter. Sprinkle garlic salt on chops each time you turn them. When chops are done, remove foil from grill. Place chops back on grill and sprinkle with garlic salt each time you turn them until charcoal black.

Barbecued Ribs

Red Wine sufficient to cove ribs in a marinade 1 1/2 c Water
1 cup Currant or plum jelly or jam
1/2 Brown sugar
1/4 md Onions, finely diced
1/8 tsp.cloves
1/2 tsp.dry mustard 1/2 tsp. garlic powder 1/2 ts Salt
6 lb. Moose ribs with some loin meat attached
Freshly ground black pepper to taste

Preheat oven to 325 degrees. Combine all ingredients except the ribs in a large bowl. Blend well. Sprinkle ribs with pepper and additional salt. Place in 5 qt. roasting pan in double layer. Roast 1 hour. Pour sauce over ribs. Increase heat to 350 degrees and bake until ribs just begin to char on top, about 1 1/2 hours. Turn ribs over cover pan and bake about 30 minutes longer, until ribs are tender and sauce is thick. To serve, place ribs on serving platter. Pour sauce over ribs. Makes about 6 servings. >

Note: If Moose is a little gamey tasting, increase vinegar in sauce to 3 tbsp. Taste sauce after mixing and add additional brown sugar to taste, about 1/2 cup.

Moose Tenderloin

1 lb. Moose tenderloin
1/2 tsp. ground thyme
1/4 tsp. ground nutmeg
1 tsp. black pepper
1/2 cup soy sauce
1 cup hickory chips
5 lb. of charcoal
Blackberry Sauce
parsley sprigs
radish rosettes
yellow squash slices

Mix thyme, nutmeg, pepper and soy sauce, and marinate Moose tenderloin overnight in buttermilk with added tenderizer in the refrigerator. Soak 1 cup of hickory chips in a bucket of water overnight.

Build a fire in a covered barbecue grill using 5 lbs. of charcoal. Allow the coals to burn for 30 minutes. If using a gas grill, preheat for 30 minutes.

Scatter the soaked chips over the coals and close the lid and cook until meat reaches 140-140 F. The meat should be slightly pink in the center and quite moist. Serve on a platter with Blackberry Sauce. Garnish with parsley sprigs and yellow squash slices. Serves 2 to 4.

Sauted Steak

5 Moose steaks cut 1-inch thick—backstrap & tenderloin are the best
2 eggs
3/4 cup buttermilk
1 cup all-purpose flour salt & pepper seasoned salt
1/4 cup canola oil

Marinate 3 days in buttermilk. Beat eggs. Set aside. Mix all-purpose flour, salt, pepper, and seasoned salt. Dip steaks into buttermilk/egg mixture and then dredge them on both sides in the flour mixture. Saute for 5-6 minutes on medium-high heat until golden brown or desired doneness.

Moose Meat Loaf

1 lb. Ground Moose
1 8 oz Can Tomato Sauce
1 cup oatmeal
1 egg
1/2 Med Onion chopped
1/2 Med Bellpepper chopped
2 tbsp.parsley
1 tsp. salt
1 tsp.Pepper
1 tsp. sugar pinch
Rosemary sprigs

Combine all ingredients in Mix well. Press into 9x9x2 loaf pan. Cook in 350 degree oven for 25 to 30 minutes. Great served with Mashed potato's.

Moose Shoulder

5 lb. Moose shoulder
1 tsp. garlic powder
2 tbsp. Bacon Fat
4 stalks Celery
15 Baby Carrots
1 big chopped Onion
1 pint Port wine
1 tbsp. sugar
Salt and pepper to taste
1 tsp. MSG
4 cups of noodles

Directions

Pot roast Elk in bacon fat, wine, carrots, garlic and onions until the meat falls off the bone. Add water if necessary.

Remove shoulder. Allow to cool and take meat off bones. Puree vegetablers and sauce in a blender. Correct seasonings. Put cooked noodles on a serving platter. Top with meat. Top the Meat with sauce. Top the sauce with a large strawberry or similar decoration and serve.

Barbecued Moose

Red Wine sufficient to cove ribs in a marinade
1 1/2 c Water
1 cup Currant or plum jelly or jam
1/2 Brown sugar
1/4 md Onions, finely diced
1/8 tsp.cloves
1/2 tsp.dry mustard
1/2 tsp. garlic powder
1/2 ts Salt
6 lb. Moose ribs with some loin meat attached
Freshly ground black pepper to taste

Preheat oven to 325 degrees. Combine all ingredients except the ribs in a large bowl and Blend well. Sprinkle ribs with pepper and additional salt. Place in 5 qt. roasting pan in double layer. Roast 1 hour. Pour sauce over ribs. Increase heat to 350 degrees and bake until ribs just begin to char on top, about 1 1/2 hours.

Turn ribs over cover pan and bake about 30 minutes longer, until ribs are tender and sauce is thick. To serve, place ribs on serving platter. Pour sauce over ribs. Makes about 6 servings.

Note: If Moose is a little gamey tasting, increase vinegar in sauce to 3 tbsp. Taste sauce after mixing and add additional brown sugar to taste, about 1/2 cup.

Moose Chops

6 Moose chops, cut 1 1/4" to 1 1/2" thick
1 1/2 cups garlic croutons
1/2 cup apple, chopped
1/2 cup Cheddar cheese, shredded
2 Tbsp. raisins
2 Tbsp. Butter, melted
2 Tbsp. orange juice
1/4 tsp. salt
1/8 tsp. cinnamon
Apple-Orange Cranberry Liqueur Sauce

Preheat oven to 350 degrees. Cut a pocket in the side of each Moose chop. Mix together the croutons, apple, cheese and currants. In another bowl, combine melted Butter, orange juice, salt and cinnamon. Pour butter mixture over the crouton mixture and mix gently. Lightly stuff the Moose chops with the butter-crouton mixture.

Place the stuffed chops in a shallow baking pan and bake uncovered for 1 hour. Cover with aluminum foil and bake for another 15 minutes. Serve with Apple-Orange Cranberry Liqueur Sauce. Serves 6.

Sauted Moose

3 lbs. Moose slices
1 cup flour
1 medium onion
5 tbsp. butter
1 chopped bell pepper
8 ounces sliced mushrooms
1/2 cup Sherry. Wine
1 pack Peppercorn Gravy Mix
Salt & Pepper
Garlic Pepper

In a cooking pot with a lid heat olive oil over medium heat. Season meat with salt, pepper and Garlic pepper and anything else you like to season your meat with. Mix Peppercorn Gravy Mix with flour. Then flour meat and cook until lightly brown (don't overcook). Set aside sauted meat on paper towels to absorb excess grease.

Saute chopped onion, bell pepper and mushrooms in olive oil that is left in pan. Now pour off all grease except for about 2 Tbsp. Turn heat on medium/low and add 5 or 6 Tbsp. of flour. Stir flour in pan with fork vigorously. Now with heat on medium/low stir in 2 cups of water or enough water to make desired gravy consistency. It is now time to turn heat down to low and add cooking wine, salt and pepper to taste. Place all meat back in the pan and place covered in oven on 250 degrees. Take a break and come back in 30 or an hour, Loosen your belt and say the blessing.

Crown Roast of Moose

1 or 2 whole Moose rib sections with backstraps attached
1/2 tsp. garlic salt
1/8 tsp. black pepper
1 lb. to 3 lb. Moose and Bacon Burger
1 can (20 oz.) apple slices with juice, chopped
1/3 cup apple cider
10 slices dried bread; cut into 1/2 inch cubes
2 Tbsp. raisins
3/4 tsp. salt
1 tsp. cinnamon
1/2 tsp. cardamom
1/4 tsp. allspice
Apple-Orange Cranberry Liqueur Sauce

Note: The assembly of the crown is difficult. It is recommended that you take two whole rib sections, with backstraps still attached, to a butcher and have them to assemble the crown roast.

If you would like to try to assemble your own. Cut off rib tips even and about 6" above the backbone. Place the two rib roasts end to end on meat board. Cut two small slits behind the adjoining ribs and tie together with cotton twine. Cut two small slits on the end ribs; pull together, meat side toward center, and tie, forming a crown roast. Or, pull both ends of 12 rib roast in to a circle and tie forming a crown.

Mix garlic salt and pepper together; rub mixture into all sides of roast. Place seasoned roast, bone ends up, in a shallow roasting pan. Cook Garlic Moose Sausage in a skillet until brown, drain excess grease. Combine next eight ingredients with sausage, stir enough to moisten dried bread. Fill center of crown roast with sausage mixture; cover with aluminum foil. Insert meat thermometer into center of roast. Bake at 325 degrees for two or three hours or until meat thermometer reads 135 degrees to 140 degrees. (Time varies according to size and age of animal.) Add decorative frills for the top of each crown point, (available a local butcher shop.) Serve with Apple-Orange Cranberry Liqueur Sauce. Serves 10 to 14.

Barbecued Chops

20 Moose chops
6 oz Italian Salad Dressing
1 lg Onion, chopped
2 ounces sugar
2 oz Garlic

Place aluminum foil on hot grill with sides folded up, so there is no runoff of juices. Place chops on foil. Add salad dressing, chopped onion and sugar. Sprinkle garlic salt on chops each time you turn them. When chops are done, remove foil from grill. Place chops back on grill and sprinkle with garlic salt each time you turn them until charcoal black.

Moose Salisbury Steak

5 backstrap, tenderloin, or shoulder steaks—Elk, deer, moose or Antelope will all work fine
2 large onions, cut into thin, long strips
4 large, fresh tomatoes, or two 8-oz. cans whole, peeled tomatoes
1/4 cup olive oil salt & pepper
worchestershire sauce

Heat oil in large saucepan and heat steaks on both sides. Add rest of ingredients. Cover, turn heat to medium-low and simmer for 30-45 minutes. Serve fresh over a hot bed of rice or noodles, or just eat plain. Delicious.

Moose Tid Bits

2 Moose backstraps
2 cups all-purpose flour
2 Tbsp. granulated garlic
Salt & Pepper to taste

Heat the bacon drippings in a deep fryer until hot. Combine all dry ingredients in a brown paper bag and shake well to mix. Slice backstraps into 1.5" wide strips. Place Moose strips in bag and shake to cover well with the dry ingredients. Deep fry the floured strips until slightly darker than golden brown. Serve on a platter with your favorite drink.

Moose Wok Stir Fry

One large Chinese Wok skillet
2 cups small strips of Moose
2 tbsp. canola or olive oil
1 large clove garlic, crushed
1 cup chopped green peppers
2 cups sliced mushrooms
1 cup diced onion
1 cup cubed potatoes
1 cup corn kernels (frozen work well)
1/3 cup worchestershire sauce
1/3 cup red wine vinegar salt & pepper
crushed oregano leaves

Heat oil in wok until very hot. Add crushed garlic clove and let sizzle a minute or so. Add Moose strips and saute for a few minutes. Add potatoes and onions next and saute for about 5 minutes, stirring every so often.

Add worchestershire sauce and red wine vinegar. Add salt, pepper and oregano leaves as needed to taste. Lastly, add green peppers, mushrooms and corn kernels, and cook only long enough that vegetables don't go limp. Tastes great with a topping of freshly grated parmesan cheese.

Moose Picante #2

2-3 lbs. of Moose with fat trimmed away
1 cup Soy Sauce
1 cup Worcestershire Sauce
2 oz. liquid smoke flavor
1 tbsp. garlic powder
2 tsp.Chili Powder
1 large mixing bowl

Directions

Set oven to 170 F
Prepare marinade mixture: Add Soy Sauce, Worcestershire Sauce, smoke flavoring, chili Powder, Chili powder and garlic powder to a large mixing bowl and stir. Cut meat into strips about 1/4 inch thick. Remove as much of the strong tasting fat as you can. Place strips in the marinade and stir. Cover bowl and store in the refrigerator for 24 hr.

Layer the meat strips between paper towels and press to remove excess marinade. Once the strips have been pressed, place them in the oven until strips are thoroughly dry, usually 3-4 hours.

Moose Backstrap

1 Backstrap/2 Tenderloin
1/2 Cup Red Wine
1/2 Cup Water
1 Onion
1 Bell Pepper
16 oz. Mushrooms
Flour
One half Cup Butter (about)
1 to 1 1/2 cups uncooked rice

Start rice when you begin cooking, everything should be ready at the same time. Marinate meat in your favorite marinade for 4 to 24 hours. Cut meat into 1/2 inch cubes, flour, heat on low with butter in a large skillet or large pot (needs to be large enough for all contents), and set aside.
Cut up all vegetables and brown in remaining butter.
Add wine, water, and meat.
Cook until it starts to thicken (Note: add a little cornstarch mix with COLD water to help thicken if needed). Serve over rice, serves 2 to 4 people.

Moose Roll Ups

Backstrap or other tender Moose cut, cut into strips about 2-3" wide and 4" long
Bacon
Italian dressing
Fresh pablano peppers cut into thin strips
Jack cheese cut into 1/2" x 1/2" slices
Toothpicks

Pound back strap strips to about 1/4" thick. Marinate back strap over night in Italian salad dressing. Lay out one strip of bacon. Place one back strap strip on bacon. Place one pepper strip on back strap.
Place cheese inside pepper strip. Roll tightly and secure with toothpick. Cool over coals until bacon is done.

Moose Casserole

2 lb. Ground Moose, beef
8-10 slices of bacon
2 cans of tomato soup (un-diluted)
2 cans of whole kernel corn
1 Med. Onion (chopped)
1 Tsp. Garlic Powder
1 pkg. Chili seasoning
2 boxes of Jiffy cornbread mix

In a large skillet cook bacon, remove bacon and drain on paper towel, save drippings. Brown hamburger and onions in drippings. Add the 2 cans of tomato soup, and chili seasoning on top of other ingredients.
Mix corn. bacon crush Or strips. the in layer Then cans 2 dish. baking 9x14 hamburger simmering,
After minutes. ten about for simmer Let Bake @ 350 degree oven until corn bread mix is golden brown.

Moose Jerky

4 lb. moose roast
2 Tbsp. Worcestershire sauce
1/4 cup salt
1/4 cup brown sugar
2 cups beer
1 cup apple cider
4 ounces soy sauce
1/4 cup whiskey
1/2 tsp. onion powder
1 tsp. garlic powder
1 tsp. ginger powder
2 teaspoons orange zest

Cut roast into slices 1/4 inch thick by 1 to 2 inches wide. Place meat in marinade, made by combining above ingredients in glass or ceramic bowl. Marinate for at least 24 to 36 hours in a cool place. Remove to wire rack and allow to air dry until glazed. (about 45 minutes). Use hickory chips soaked in water and added to coals to smoke the jerky 12 to 16 hours at 150 to 175 degrees.

Barbecued Ribs

6 lb. Moose ribs with some loin meat
Red Wine sufficient to cove ribs in a marinade
1 1/2 c Water
1 cup Currant or plum jelly or jam
1/2 Brown sugar
1/4 medium Onions, finely diced
1/8 tsp. cloves
1/2 tsp. dry mustard
1/2 tsp. garlic powder
1/2 tsp. Salt
Freshly ground black pepper to taste

Marinate Moose in buttermilk overnight. Preheat oven to 325 degrees. Combine all ingredients except the ribs in a large bowl. Blend well. Sprinkle ribs with pepper and additional salt. Place in 5 qt. roasting pan in double layer. Roast 1 hour. Pour sauce over ribs. Increase heat to 350 degrees and bake until ribs just begin to char on top, about 1 1/2 hours.

Turn ribs over cover pan and bake about 30 minutes longer, until ribs are tender and sauce is thick. To serve, place ribs on serving platter. Pour sauce over ribs. Makes about 6 servings.

MUSKRAT RECIPES

Muskrat with Onions

One muskrat, cleaned and quartered
One half tsp. Salt and Pepper
1/4 tsp. paprika
1/2 cup flour
3 tbsp. Bacon fat
3 large onions
1 cup sour cream

Soak muskrat overnight in buttermilk to soften meat and remove gamey flavor. Season with 1 tsp. Salt, pepper and paprika, roll in flour, and saute in bacon fat until browned. Cover muskrat with onions, sprinkle onions with 1/2 tsp. salt. Pour in the cream. Cover skillet tightly and simmer for 1 hour. Serves 4.

Sauteed Muskrat

One muskrat
Water
1 tsp. salt
1/8 tsp. pepper
1/2 med. sliced onion
1/4 cup bacon fat
1 chopped onion
1/2 cup chopped clelery
1 can Italian or stewed tomatoes
1/2 tsp. Worcestershire Sauce

Soak muskrat overnight in buttermilk. Wash and clean thoroughly. Then disjoint, and cut into desired pieces. Place in a deep pan and add 1 quart water, salt, pepper, and onion. Cook about 1 hour. Melt fat in skillet and fry meat to brown on one side. Turn and immediately put in vegetables and Worcestershire Sauce. Almost cover with water (about 1 cup) and let simmer until tender (about 30 minutes).

Muskrat Meat Loaf

1 1/2 lbs. ground muskrat
Water
1/4 tsp. thyme
1 tsp. salt
2 beaten eggs
1 chopped onion
1 tsp. Garlic powder 1/2 cup instant oatmeal
1/4 tsp. pepper
1 tsp. Oregano

Soak muskrat overnight in buttermilk. Wash and clean thoroughly. Then remove meat from bones, and grind. Mix ground meat thoroughly with other ingredients. Place in meat loaf dish. Place dish in pan containing hot water. Bake in moderate oven (350 degrees) for 1 1/4-2 hours. Serves 6-8.

Stuffed Muskrat

1 muskrat
3 med. potatoes
2 tbsp. butter
1 1/2 tsp. salt
1/4 tsp. pepper
1 tsp. dried summer savory
1 cup finely chopped celery
2 large carrots
3 slices bacon

Clean and soak muskrat overnight buttermilk. Cook potatoes and mash potatoes with the butter, season with 1/2 tsp. salt, 1/8 tsp. pepper, savory, and celery. Fill the muskrat with this stuffing and sew it up.

Rub muskrat with 1 tsp. salt and 1/8 tsp.pepper. Place on a rack in a roasting pan with he legs tied under the body. Place two large quartered carrots on the rack beside the muskrat. Place bacon on the back. Bake in a hot oven (400 degrees F).

After 10 minutes, pour two cups of hot water over the body and continue cooking for 45 minutes. Remove bacon the last 10 minutes to brown the back. Serves 4.

PARTRIDGE RECIPES

Braised Partridges

4 Partridges
1 forked egg
2 tbsp. Bacon fat
1/2 cup chopped Onion
1 tsp. Garlic powder
Salt and pepper to taste
1 tsp. MSG
1/2 cup Port wine

Directions

Mix all ingredients except Port Wine in a covered pot. Simmer for 45 minute or until tender. Add water when necessary.

Deglaze pan with Port Wine to make a wine sauce

Hunter's Partridge Stew

4 Partridges
15 baby carrots
1 cup diced celery
4 slices of crumbled bacon
1 cup Chicken broth
1/2 tsp. thyme
1/2 tsp. tarragon
Salt and pepper to taste
1 tsp. MSG

Put all ingredients in a pot and simmer for 1 hour.

Serve with small paste like shells or rotini.

Mexican Partridge

Ingredients

4 Partridges
12 baby carrots
1 cup diced celery
2 tbsp. Bacon Fat
1 can Chicken soup
1 1/2 cups milk
1 tbsp. chili powder
1 jar medium Salsa
1 tsp. MSG

Directions

Put all ingredients in a pot and stir until mixed. Seal cover of pot with aluminum foil. Simmer gently for 45 minutes. Check to add moisture (wine) if needed and to adjust seasonings

Italian Style Partridge

Ingredients

6 Partridges
2 tsp. garlic salt
1 tsp. Powdered Oregano
1 tsp. Salt
1/2 tsp. Pepper
2 cups Port wine
2 tsp. Parmesan cheese
1 tsp. MSG

Directions

Put all ingredients in a pot. Stir well. Seal edges with foil and simmer for 1 hour.

Chukar Partridge Recipe

5 Chukar partridges
Salt and Pepperto taste
2 tbsp. Baconf Fat
1 2 tsp. Garlic powder
1 tbsp. Paprika
1 tbsp. Dill
1 chopped medium onion
3 lg Green Peppers, chopped fine
1 cup sweet (cookling) Sherry
1 cup Water
1 tbsp. flour

Directions

Use a large pot. Saute partridges in bacon fat, turning thm over in the pot. When toasted, add the remainder of the ingredients and seal the top with foil and simmer for 1 hour.

Check to see if pot needs more moisture and if seasonings need adjusting.

At the end, thicken with cornstarch if desired.

PHEASANT RECIPES

Roast Pheasant

1 pheasant
1 tsp. salt
1/4 tsp. pepper
1 bay leaf
3 stalks celery
1/3 cup melted butter
6 bacon slices
1 med. onion
1 (3 oz.) can mushrooms
1 chicken bouillon cube
1/2 cup Irish Cream Whiskey
One half cup heavy cream
Seedless Grapes
Wild rice

Sprinkle salt and pepper on pheasant. Put onion, mushrooms and celery in bird's cavity. Place breast side down on a rack in the roasting pan. Dribble melted butter over breast and place bacon strips on top of bird. Mix onion, mushrooms, and reconstituted bouillon cube together and pour into bottom of roasting pan.

Pheasant Roast #2

Six pheasant breasts salt
Pepper
Flour
Cooking Oil
30 grapes
2 cans of mushroom soup
1 cup heavy cream
2 ounces Brandy
1 tsp. sugar

Preheat oven to 350 degrees F. Sprinkle seasoned salt and pepper on Pheasant breasts and flour them. Brown lightly in a skillet with cooking oil; then put in a greased baking dish and set aside. Combine the 2 cans of soup in a saucepan with the heavy cream and heat. Add the grapes. Pour soup mixture over pheasant and bake 1 hour. Mix in brandy befor serving. Also good with Dove and quail.

Pheasant with Sour Cream

One pheasant
Flour
Salt and pepper
1 pint sour cream
1 onion
1 box sliced mushrooms
1 chopped green or red bell pepper

Clean and wash pheasant; cut into quarters and marinate in buttermilk with added meat tenderizer. Wash off buttermilk and wipe thoroughly. Next dip in flour and brown gently in butter in a frying pan. Deglaze pan with a small amount of water. Place this with pheasant in a roasting pan and sprinkle with salt and pepper. Put enough sour cream in pan to make its depth 1 inch and add 1/8 lb. of butter for each bird. Cover and bake at 350 degrees F. for 3/4 hrs. or until bird are tender. Add milk to sour cream as needed to maintain consistency.

Saute the onion, the chopped pepper and in olive oil. Add to sour cream and cover birds before serving. Serve pheasant with accouterments

Braised Pheasant

1 pheasant, cleaned and quartered
1 med. onion, cut into pieces
2 stalks celery, chopped
6 small carrots
2 ounces of ham
1 tsp. sugar
Salt and pepper to taste
1 tsp. MSG
4 ounces of sherry

Make a broth using canned chicken broth onion, celery, carrots and ham.

Brush pheasant with bacon fat and brown in a pot roat pot.

Add broth and contents and cook for 1 hour or until tender.

Remove bird and blend liquid in a blender.

Add broth and contents to the pan used to brown bird and let it simmer 2-3 minutes. If there isn't enough broth, add water. Add sherry to sauce, place bird on platter and pour sauce over meat.

Italian Pheasant

1 pheasant, quartered and cleaned
1 medium chopped onion
2 green peppers i/2 tsp. garlic powder
1 tbsp. sesame oil
1 tsp. salt
1/4 cup olive oil i jar spaghetti sauce
One half cup parmesan cheese
1 tbsp. sugar
1 tsp. oregano salt and pepper to taste

Brown turkey pieces very gently. Deglaze pan; mix vegetables, seasonings and spaghetti sauce, and parmesan cheese sauce in a pot: add pheasant with deglazed juices. Simmer till done adding water if necessary.

Apricot Pheasant

One pheasant cleaned and washed
1 onion cut up
6 baby carrots
3 stalks of celery chopped
1 apple chopped
Salt and pepper

Wash bird. Stuff bird with apple, carrots, celery, and onion. You may cook the birds slowly at 350 degrees F or quickly at 450 degrees F. Be sure to baste often with a mixture of butter and wine or butter and broth. The time required will depend on the size of the bird and the desired amount of doneness. Geese will require 20-30 minutes at 450 degrees F. and 1 to 1 1/2 hours at 350 degrees

While Pheasant is cooking make a sauce of one jar of apricot preserves with added canned or dried appricots
1 tbsp. brandy

Pheasant and Wild Rice

1 cup raw wild rice
1 can cream of chicken soup
1 can cream of mushroom soup
1 can mushrooms
2 1/2 cups water
Water chestnuts
2 pheasants, cut up, floured and browned
1 pkg. instant onion soup mix

Mix rice, canned soups, water, mushrooms and water chestnuts in 9x13 glass casserole. Add pheasant. Sprinkle with onion soup mix. Cover lightly with foil. Bake 2-2 1/2 hours at 300 degrees.

Pheasant a la Creme

2 pheasants
Salt, pepper and paprika
1/2 cup butter
2 cups sour cream
2 tab. dry sherry
1/2 lb. fresh mushrooms, sliced
1 onion, finely chopped
1/2 cup finely chopped celery
1/2 cup sliced olives
2 tab. chopped pimentos

Quarter birds. Sprinkle with salt, pepper and paprika. Dredge with flour.

Brown in butter. Remove birds and place in roasting pan. Add remaining ingredients to butter in which birds were browned and stir until mixed and warmed. Pour over pheasants. Cover and bake at 300 degrees for 2 hours.

Honey Baked Pheasant

Legs and breast of 1 pheasant, skinned
1/2 cup flour
1/2 cup chopped parsley
2 cups honey
1 cup butter salt and pepper to taste

Fillet breast and bone the thighs. Cut into approx. same thickness pieces.

Season the flour with salt and pepper and dredge the pheasant. Dust pheasant pieces with onion powder. Melt 3/4 cup butter in skillet over medium heat. Brown pheasant pieces and place in a lightly oiled 9x13 glass casserole. Sprinkle with parsley. Add honey and 1/4 cup butter to the skillet. Mix well until butter is melted, then pour over the pheasant (should come about halfway up on the pheasant pieces). Seal the baking dish with aluminum foil and bake 30 minutes at 325 degrees.

Stir Fry Pheasant

1 cup buttermilk baking mix
1/2 tsp. pepper
3/4-1 lb. diced uncooked pheasant (or other upland bird)
2 eggs, slightly beaten
1 tab peanut oil
3 medium carrots, cut diagonally into 1/2 inch pieces
1 green pepper, cut into strips
1 small onion, thinly sliced and separated into rings
2 tabs water
3 tabs peanut oil
3/4 cup chicken broth
2 tabs teriyaki sauce
Hot cooked rice

Directions

In large plastic bag, combine baking mix and pepper; shake to mix. Set aside. Combine pheasant meat and eggs; stir to coat meat with egg. Put pieces of pheasant in plastic bag and shake to coat. In wok or large skillet, heat 1 tabs oil over medium high heat until hot. Add carrots; cook and stir for about 2 minutes. Add green pepper and onion. Cook and stir for 1 minute longer. Add water; cover.

Steam for 3-4 minutes, until vegetables are tender-crisp. Remove vegetables from wok and keep warm. Add 3 tabs oil to wok; heat over medium heat until hot. Add pheasant; cook and stir until golden brown and no longer pink in center. Combine chicken broth and teriyaki sauce; pour over meat. Return vegetables to wok, cook and stir until heated through. Serve with rice.

Pheasant Paprika

Ingredients

2-3 lbs. pheasant pieces
8 slices bacon, cut up
2 tbsp. Flour
2 tbsp. paprika
1/4 cup chopped onion
1 1/2 tsp. salt
1 cup of chicken broth
1 pkg. White Sauce or Bechamel
1-1 1/2 cups sour cream
Hot cooked egg noodles

Directions

In medium skillet, cook bacon over medium heat until it just begins to brown. Add onion. Cook and stir until onion is tender. Remove from heat.

Remove bacon and onion from skillet; set aside; reserve drippings.

In large plastic food storage bag, combine flour, 1 1/2 tsp. paprika and salt; shake to mix. Add pheasant, a few piece at a time, to bag,

Saute pheasant in bacon fat. Add chicken broth, reduce heat; cover and simmer until tender, 25 to 40 minutes, adding the additional broth to pan during cooking if necessary.

Prepare sauce according to package directions using Bacon fat instead of butter and Chickenb stock instead of milk. Add paprika and reserved bacon and onion. Cover and simmer until thickened.

Remove from heat; skim fat. Put the pheasant on the serving platter and keep warm. Stir in sour cream into saauce mixture in skillet. Cook over low heat until just heated; do not boil. Pour sauce over pheasant. Serve with hot cooked egg noodles.

QUAIL RECIPES

Quail in Plum Sauce

(can be used with chicken)

Ingredients

10 quail
4 tbsp. Olive Oil
6 depitted plums
4 oz. Heavy cream
Salt, Pepper and Accent to taste
4 oz. port wine

Directions

Saute quail just like chicken. Add plums, wine, simmer for 1 minute and deglaze pan Strain liquids into blender

Depit 6 plums. Add salt, pepper, MSG and blend on high with cream

Transfer to a serving dish. Decorate and serve

Quail in Sweet and Sour Sauce

Ingredients

12 Quail
4 tbsp. Butter
1 tsp. Garlic Powder
Salt and Pepper to taste

Saute quail as you would chicken in butter, salt, pepper and garlic powder

Sauce

Ingredients:

Sweet and sour sauce

1 cup sugar
1/2 cup water
1/2 cup white vinegar
2 tbsp. cornstarch
2 tbsp. honey mustard
1 tsp. Garlic powder
2 tbsp. catsup

Combine all ingredients making sure the cornstarch is thoroughly dissolved. Cook over low heat till sugar et al is desolved and thickened.

Quail and Artichokes

3 lbs. quail or Dove
1 1/2 tsp. salt
1/2 tsp. pepper
1/2 tsp. paprika
6 tbsp. butter
15 oz. can artichokes
1/4 lb. mushrooms
2 tbsp. flour
2/3 cup chicken consomme
3-4 tbsp. sherry
Salt, pepper, and paprika

Directions

Saute quail or Dove in 4 tbsp. butter. Place in casserole. Place artichokes between quail or Dove. Saute mushrooms in 2 tbsp. butter. Add 2 tbsp. flour. Stir in consomme and sherry. Cook 5 minutes. Pour over quail or Dove.

Cover and cook at 350 degrees for 1 hour.

Baked Quail

12-18 quail or Dove breasts
1 med. onion, chopped
1 box sliced mushrooms
2 tbsp. melted butter or margarine
Salt and pepper
1 can cream of celery soup—undiluted
1/2 tsp. Oregano
1 (4 oz.) can mushrooms, drained
1/2 tsp. Rosemary
1/2 cup Sherry
1 cup sour cream
Cooked wild rice

Arrange quail in a large baking dish—do not crowd. Saute onion and mushrooms in butter, add remaining ingredients except sour cream and rice. Pour over quail and cover dish. Bake at 325 degrees for 1 hour, turning quail occasionally. Add sour cream and stir into sauce.

Leave uncovered and bake an additional 20 minutes. Spoon sauce over rice.

Italian Quail

12-18 quail breasts
1 med. onion, chopped
1 box sliced mushrooms
2 tbsp. melted butter or margarine
Salt and pepper
1 jar Favorite Pasta Sauce
1 tsp. Oregano
1 (4 oz.) can mushrooms, drained
1/2 tsp. Rosemary
1/2 cup Port wine
Cooked rice

Arrange quail in a large baking dish—do not crowd. Saute onion and mushrooms in butter, add remaining ingredients and rice. Pour over quail and cover dish.

Bake at 325 degrees for 1 hour, turning quail occasionally. Leave uncovered and bake an additional 20 minutes. Spoon sauce over rice.

Creamed Qauil with Brandy

9 quail
1 tsp. Salt
1/2 tsp. Pepper
2 sticks butter
2 cups heavy cream
1 tsp. Thyme
3 tbsp. Brandy
1/2 cup toasted bread crumbs

Clean and split quail. Salt and pepper birds and simmer in butter in frying pan until tender. Add cream and sprinkle Thyme over birds, and continue to cook until done. Add brandy and garnish with bread crumbs.

Yields: 4-6 servings.

Quail Amandine

6 Quail split down back
1/4 cup flour
Salt and pepper
4 tbsp. butter
1/2 cup red table wine
1 tbsp. sugar
1/2 cup blanched, sliced almonds

Dust birds in flour seasoned with salt and pepper. Melt butter and sauté birds until nicely browned. Add wine and sugar. Cover and continue cooking slowly for 15-20 minutes. Add almonds and cook for 5-10 minutes longer or until birds are fork tender. (Allow 2 quail or woodcock per serving; 4 Dove or snipe.)

Quail and Rice

12 quail
4 large onions
1 stalk celery
2 cans chopped mushrooms
2 cups uncooked Rice
Salt and pepper to taste
2 cups chicken stock

Split quail. Cut onions, mushrooms and celery and cook in butter until tender. Put in a large baking pan or Dutch oven and add the quail, chicken broth rice and salt and pepper; stir.

Place in 350 degrees F. oven and cook until tender. Add more liquid as needed.

Quail Casserole

8-12 quail
Salt
Flour pepper
One half tsp. Thyme
One half tsp. Sage
1/3 cup Olive oil or butter
1/2 lb. fresh mushrooms or 4-oz. can sliced mushrooms
1 tsp. Thyme
2 cups dry sherry

Preheat oven to 350 degrees F. Split birds down back. Add salt to the flour and dust birds lightly.

Saute Birds until browned on both sides. Remove birds from skillet and place in a casserole dish with lid. Add mushrooms seasonings and thyme and pour enough sherry into casserole to half cover the birds. Cover casserole and heat in oven for 1 hour. Spoon the clear sherry gravy over the birds before serving. Serves 4-6 people.

Easy Quail with Wild Rice

Ingredients

10 quail, split into halves
One box Uncle Ben's Wild Rice mix
4 cups water
1 can cream of mushroom soup

Directions

Preheat oven to 350 degrees F.

Put rice in bottom of baking dish. Place quail on top. Add cream of mushroom soup and water. Sprinkle onion soup mix on top. Cook covered for 2 hours.

Add water as needed.

Easy Dutch Oven Quail

Ingredients

12 Quail
1/2 cup flour
1/2 cup Cornmeal
4 tbsp. Bacon fat
1 cup Sherry
2 tsp. Salt
1 tsp. pepper

Directions

Roll quail in combination of flour and cornmeal. Have a moderate amount of fat piping hot in Dutch oven. Brown birds quickly on both sides. Then add a little water, sherry and the seasonings and turn fire low to let simmer for one hour.

Pot Roast Quail with Mushrooms

Ingredients

12 Quail
12 Bacon
2 tsp. salt
1 tsp. Pepper
Sugar
2 cups Mushrooms
1 cup Sherry
1 medium minced onion Onions
2 tsp. Sage

Directions

Parboil birds. Then wrap each bird with a slice of bacon and put them into a buttered pot to simmer with some sherry, onions, garlic and sage.

Baste occasionally while they are roasting.

If they are large birds, they will take about 1/2 hour to cook. When they are done, put them into a warmer for 2 minutes while you add 1 tbsp. of butter, a little fresh sherry stirring to make gravy.

Serve the birds on toat with he gravy poured over them; garnish with warm hearts of artichoke grape jelly. On the same plate, serve mushrooms as follows:

Sautéed Quail

Bookmark this valuable site

8 Quail
1/4 cup Flour
1 tsp. Garlic powder tbsp. Bacon Fat
1 cup Port wine
1 tsp. Pepper
1 tsp. Tarragon

Parboil quail. Sprinkle salt and pepper on the bird and and dredge it with flour. Saute quail in hot fat and brown quickly.

Cover pan, add seasonings and reduce heat. Cook slowly until tender, turning the quail occasionally. Deglaze pan with red wine and simmer to make a gravy.

Serve on hot platter garnished with thin slices of lemon and sprig of parsley.

Easy Dutch Oven Quail

Ingredients

10 quail, split and washed
4 cups water
20 Carrots
1 1/2 cups long grain rice (uncooked)
1 pkg. dried onion soup mix
1 tsp. Garlic Powder
2 cups Port wine

Directions

Place rice in bottom of a Dutch Oven; add quail. Spoon mushroom soup over birds. Add water and sprinkle with onion soup mix. Cover pan and seal edges with Aluminum. Bake 2 hours at 350 degrees F. Uncover last 10 minutes to brown. There is no need to add salt and pepper as mushroom and onion soup mix contain adequate seasoning. Serves 5.

Quail Chili

One pound of quail
3 lbs. dry kidney or pinto beans, cooked or 32 oz. canned beans
2 regular sixe cans stewed tomatoes
1 large chopped
4 tsp. garlic powder
1 tsp. salt
1 cup water
2 tbsp.Chile Powder
2 tbsp. Cumin
Salt
1 tbsp. chili Powder
2 tsp. MSG

Put cooked beans into large pot; add Quail, tomatoes, chil powder, cumin, onion, salt, garlic, and MSG. Simmer fo 30 minutes to heat thoroughly.

Quail in Port Wine

Ingredients

6 quail, cleaned
1 tbsp. Brandy
6 tbsp. butter or margarine
2 cups sliced mushrooms
I large chopped onion
1/4 cup melted butter or margarine
1 cup consomme
1 cup dry Port wine
1 stalk celery, quartered
Salt and pepper
Juice of 2 oranges, strained

Directions

Dust Quail with flour. Saute the Quail in butter and add onions and the mushrooms and onion. Add consomme, Port, celery, salt, and pepper.

Cover and simmer 20-30 minutes or until quail is tender. Stir in Brandy and orange juice and heat thoroughly.

Quail au Vin Blanc

6 quail, cleaned and cut into serving pieces
1/4 cup olive oil
1 onion, chopped
1/2 half tsp. thyme
1/2 tsp. tarragon
1 tbsp. chives, chopped
1/2 tsp. pepper
1 tsp. Garlic powder
2 cups white wine
1 tsp. Salt
2 cups heavy cream

Use a pot with a cover. Saute quail in olive oil. Add onion, chives, peppercorns and garlic and simmer for 3 minutes. Add quail and brown.

Add wine, salt, pepper, tarragon, thyme and chives. Simmer 45 minutes or until tender. Remove quail to a servuing platterand keep warm. Add cream to sauce. Simmer until thickened and pour over Quail.

Quail a l'Orange

15 quail, cleaned and washed
Salt
Pepper
All-purpose flour
8 slices bacon
4 tsp. Garlic powder
1 cup milk
I can Frozen Orange Juice
1 cup heavy cream
1 tbsp. MSG.

Sprinkle Quail with salt and pepper to taste; dredge in flour, and set aside.

Saute bacon until crisp in a large skillet. Remove bacon, reserve for other uses. Add Quail and cook 10-12 minutes on each side or until done.

Pour off bacon fat.

Blend together orange juice, cream, sugar, garlic powder and MSG. Pour into pan. Heat until thickened. Check seasonings. Put Quail on a serving dish, cover with sauce and serve.

Quail for a King

Ingredients

6 quail, cleaned
1/2 tsp. salt
1/2 tsp. pepper
1/3 cup all-purpose flour
6 tbsp. olive oill
2 1/2 cups chicken broth
1/4 tsp.ground cinnamon
1 tbsp.of brown sugar
1 tsp. Garlic powder
8 baby carrots
2 stalks chopped celery
1/4 lb. mushrooms
1 small onion
1/2 cup sherry
1 tsp. MSG

Sprinkle quail with salt and pepper; dredge in flour. Gentley saute Quail on both sides in oil.

Add all remaining ingredients Except for Sherry. Cover the pot and simmer for 45 minutes. Add water if necessary.

Remove vegetables and blend on high with stock. Return vegetables, add sherry and simmer until the Quail is very tender.

Easy Quail Breasts

Ingredients

10 quail breasts
Seasoned salt
Pepper
Flour
Cooking Oil
1 can chicken gumbo soup
1 can golden mushroom soup
1 can onion soup

Directions

Preheat oven to 350 degrees F.

Sprinkle seasoned salt and pepper on quail breasts and flour them. Saute lightly in a skillet until brown with oil.

Then put in a greased baking dish and set aside. Combine the 3 cans of soup in a saucepan and heat. Pour soup mixture over quail and bake 1 hour. Also good with Dove and pheasant.

RABBIT RECIPES

Rabbit in Plum Sauce

2 dressed Rabbits, cut in pieces
1/4 cup soy sauce
1/4 tsp. garlic powder
1/4 tsp. ground ginger
1/4 tsp. Sage one onion
2-3 stalks celery
6-7 small carrots
1 tsp. sugar

Add all ingredients to a large pot or Dutch oven. Cover with water and cook on low heat for 3 hours. Remove Rabbits. Blend vegetables to thicken gravy. Add Rabbits and gravey back to pot. Simmer for 2-3 minutes. Serve.

Rabbit in Sweet/Sour Sauce

Sweet and Sour Rabbit
Rabbit (2 1/2 lbs.), ready to cook
2 tbsp. cooking fat or oil
1 cup pineapple juice
1/4 cup vinegar
1/2 tsp. salt
1 cup pineapple pieces
1 med. green pepper, thin half slices
1 1/2 tbsp. Cornstarch
1/4 cup sugar
1/2 cup water
Flour, salt, and pepper

Cut rabbit into serving pieces. Roll in mixture of flour, salt, and pepper.

Heat fat or oil in a pan; brown rabbit pieces on all sides over moderate heat. Add pineapple juice, vinegar, and salt. Cover pan; cook over low heat 40 minutes or until meat is tender. Add pineapple and green pepper; cook a few minutes longer. Mix cornstarch and sugar and stir into water. Stir this mixture gradually into liquid in pan and cook slowly about 5 minutes. Serves 6.

2 dressed rabbits cut into serving size pieces
1/4 cup soy sauce
1/4 cup water
1/4 cup firmly packed brown sugar
3 tbsp. lemon juice BR>1/4 tsp. garlic powder
1/4 tsp. ground ginger

Place squirrel halves or rabbit pieces in crock pot. Mix all ingredients in a small bowl and pour over meat. Cover and cook on low heat for 7-8 hours. To thicken gravy, use either flour or cornstarch mixed with water.

Cook on high until thickened.

Rabbit and Artichokes

1 dressed rabbit cut in pieces
1/3 cup flour
1/4 cup oil
1 1/2 tsp. Salt
1 tsp. pepper
1 cup chicken stock
1/2 tsp. Rosemary
1 tsp. lemon rind
1 med. onion, cut into rings
1/4 cup water
1/2 cup sour cream
Water
1/2 cup toasted slivered almonds

Coat rabbit pieces with flour (reserve remaining flour). Brown in heavy hot skillet, sprinkle with salt and pepper. Pour chicken stock with rosemary, lemon rind, and onion over rabbit. Simmer 45 minutes. Remove rabbit pieces to warmed platter. Combine reserved flour with water and stir into broth until sauce is thick. Stir in sour cream and almonds; pour over rabbit.

Rabbit and Wild Rice

Put dressed rabbit in large browning bag with McCormick's seasoning for chicken. Roast 30 minutes in microwave

Italian Rabbit

1 frozen dressed rabbit
1 large onion, cut-up
1 small green pepper, cut-up
1-2 stalks celery, sliced
2 cloves garlic, chopped
Salt and pepper
1/2 tsp. Oregano
1 tbsp. dried parsley
1-2 carrots, cut-up
3 tbsp. catsup or tomato paste
1 cup liquid (white wine, cider, tomato sauce, or water)
10 small russet potatoes

Marinade in buttermilk overnight in the frig

Defrost rabbit meat overnight and marinate. Brown rabbit with vegetables in hot skillet for 5-10 minutes. Place rabbit and other ingredients in crock pot. Cover and cook on low 3-4 hours. Serves 4-6. Cook potatoes separately and serve with rabbit

Creamed Rabbit

1-2 dressed rabbits
1/2 cup chopped celery
1/2 cup pickle cubes
3 boiled eggs, chopped
1 tsp. Salt
1 tsp. Pepper
1 tsp. Sugar
1 cup Italian or vinegrette pr blue cheese dressing

Boil rabbit till tender. Reserve stock for other uses. Cut into small pieces.

Add celery, pickles, eggs, salt, pepper, sugar, and dressing; toss thoroughly until mixed. Serve on lettuce with sliced tomato and crackers.

Rabbit Amandine

1 dressed rabbit cut in pieces
1/3 cup flour
1/4 cup oil
1 1/2 tsp. Salt
1 tsp. pepper
1 cup chicken stock
1/2 tsp. Rosemary
1 tsp. lemon rind
1 med. onion, cut into rings
1/4 cup water
1/2 cup sour cream
Water
1/2 cup toasted slivered almonds

Coat rabbit pieces with flour (reserve remaining flour). Brown in heavy hot skillet, sprinkle with salt and pepper. Pour chicken stock with rosemary, lemon rind, and onion over rabbit. Simmer 45 minutes. Remove rabbit pieces to warmed platter. Combine reserved flour with water and stir into broth until sauce is thick. Stir in sour cream and almonds; pour over rabbit.

Rabbit a la Creme

Ingredients

1 rabbit cleaned, washed and ready to cook one jar good spaghetti sauce
one can red clam sauce
3/4 cup parmesan cheese
1 green pepper diced garlic powder
2 tsp. sugar I tbsp.oregano Cook rabbit in microwave.

Directions

Cut meat in pieces. Mix all ingredients in a pot and simmer for one half hour.

Rabbit and Rice

Ingredients

1/4 cup olive oil
2 tbsp. butter or margarine
1 cup chopped onions
1 1/2 cup chopped muchrooms
1 clove garlic, minced
2 tsp. Salt
1/4 tsp. Pepper
1 cup heavy cream
1 tsp. sugar
1 cup sour cream

Directions

Preheat oven to 350

Saute rabbits in a pot until brown; Cook onions and mushrooms in a pan; add to pot; Stir in garlic, salt, peppert, sugar and gradually stir in milk; cook, stirring constantly, until mixture thickens.

Place pot in oven and bake 1 hour and 10 minutes or until rabbit is fork-tender. Remove pieces to warm platter. Stir sour cream into gravy; heat, stirring constantly (do not boil). Serve gravy over rabbit. Makes 8 servings.

Rabbit Casserole

Ingredients

2 (2 lb. each) ready-to-cook wild rabbits or 1 (5-6 lb.) domestic rabbit
1 cup water
1 tsp. sugar
2 cups dry red wine
2 cups sliced onions
2 chopped carrots
2 bay leaves
1 tbsp. Sage
1 tsp.basil
1/2 tsp. coarsely ground pepper
1/2 tsp. Salt
6 bacon slices

Directions

Day before serving: In a large bowl, pour 1 cup water and 2 cups dry red wine over rabbit pieces. Add remaining ingredients except for bacon.

Cover and refrigerate overnight, turning pieces occasionally. About 3 hrs. before serving: In 12-inch skillet over medium heat, fry bacon until crisp; drain on paper towels; reserve drippings in skillet.

Meanwhile, remove rabbit pieces from wine mixture; reserve mixture. Pat pieces dry with paper towels. On waxed paper, coat rabbit pieces with flour. saute rabbit pieces in hot bacon drippings. Brown on all sides and remove to platter as they brown. Pour remaining drippings from skilled and return rabbit to skillet.

Strain wine mixture, discarding bay leaves; stir in sugar; pour over rabbit and heat to boiling. Reduce heat to low; cover and simmer 2 hours or until rabbit is fork-tender.

Remove rabbit to warm platter. Blend carrots and onions to thicken sauce. Add flour if desired. Crumble bacon on top and serve. Makes 6 servings.

Easy Rabbit w Wild Rice

Ingredients

2 wild rabbits
Water
Juice of 1 lemon
Salt, pepper, honey and nutmeg
Egg, beaten BR>Bread crumbs
Fat for frying
Parsley
Green peas
Toast

Directions

Dress and disjoint 2 rabbits. Wipe clean and parboil 10 minutes in water containing lemon juice. Pour off stock and reserve for other uses. Pat dry and season with salt, pepper, honey and very little nutmeg.

Dip in beaten egg, then in very dry bread crumbs. Fry in deep fat (have the fat hot enough so a 1-inch cube of bread is brown in 60 seconds).

Drain free of fat by holding each piece on a fork over the pan. It makes them crispy and leaves no fatty taste. Place cooked meat on a hot dish, garnish with parsley and serve with green peas and toast. Plan to serve as many people as you would from the same weight of chicken.

Easy Dutch Oven Rabbit

Ingredients

1 lbs. dry Great Northern Beans, cooked or 32 ounces canned beans
15 oz. stewed tomatoes, undrained
1 large red onion, chunked
2 tsp. garlic powder
2 tbsp.chile powder
2 tbsp. cumin
Dash salt rabbit cut into bite-size pieces, boiled or cooked in microwave
2 bell peppers in chunks

Directions

Put cooked beans into large pot; add tomatoes, cumin, chili powder, onion, salt, garlic and rabbit (or other meat). Simmer 10 minutes to heat thoroughly.

Rabbit Pot Roast

Ingredients

1 rabbit (1 1/2 to 2 lbs.)
1 cup bias-sliced celery
1 med. onion, diced
1 tsp. Garlic powder
1/2 cup Port wine
Olive oil or butter
Salt and pepper to taste
1 tsp. sugar
1 cup chicken stock
1 tsp. dried oregano, crushed
1/4 tsp. dried marjoram
1/2 cup heavy cream
2 tbsp. snipped parsley

Directions

Quarter the rabbit. Rinse rabbit well and pat dry. First use a large pot to cook the bacon until crisp and brown. Remove bacon, saute rabbit in bacon fatl for 10 minutes, turning after 5 minutes to brown evenly.

Add all other ingredients to pot. Reduce heat; cover and simmer about 45 minutes or until rabbit pieces are tender and easily pierced with a fork. Turn rabbit once during cooking. Transfer rabbit and vegetables to a platter and keep warm.

Pour off any fat. Add cream and stir until the cream thickens slightly. Pour thickened sauce over the braised rabbit.

Sprinkle with parsley and serve.

Sauteed Rabbit

Ingredients

1 Rabbit
1/2 cup Port wine
Salt and Pepper to taste
1 tsp. Garlic Powder
1/2 lemon

Rub surfaces of rabbit pieces with garlic powder, and lemon. Stuff if desired. Place on a greased rack in a shallow pan. Brush generously with melted butter or margarine and cover loosely with foil. Roast at 325 degrees F. for 1 hour (store Rabbit) 2 hours (wild rabbit).

Remove foil during last 1/2 hour to brown. Deglaze pan with Port wine to make a wine-butter sauce

Dutch Oven Rabbit

Ingredients

1 to 2 rabbits cut into quarters
1 cup red wine
1 tbsp.sugar
2 tsp. salt
1 onion, chopped
4 whole cloves
1/2 tsp. allspice
1/2 cup dark raisins
1/4 cup brown sugar

Directions

Place rabbit pieces in deep pot and cover with cool water. Add red wine and water sufficient to cover, 2 tsp. salt, onion, cloves, bay leaves, and allspice. Cook until almost tender and then add raisins and brown sugar.

Continue cooking until rabbit is tender and done. Remove rabbit from pot and thicken liquid with a roux of flour and water. Replace rabbit in thickened gravy and heat just before serving.

Rabbit Chili

1 rabbit, cut into serving-size pieces
1/2 cup flour
1/4 tsp.pepper
1 tsp. salt
1/4 cup water
4 tbsp. fat
1 onion, chopped

Roll rabbit in mixture of flour, salt, and pepper. Brown in fat. Add water, and onion. Cover and simmer until tender. Remove cover the last 10 minutes to brown.

Rabbit in Red Wine

2 rabbits, (4-6 lbs. meat) cut up
1 onion
1/2 half box sliced mushrooms
1/2 cup butter
1 tbsp. paprika
1 tsp.ground sage
1 1/2 tsp. salt
Pepper i/2 cup sherry

Saute rabbits and onions in butter until browned. In 12-inch covered pan over low heat cook rabbits with sherry, paprika, sage, garlic, salt and pepper until fork tender. Add water or more sherry if needed.

Rabbit in White Wine

Quartered Rabbit
Salt
Barbecue Sauce

Boil rabbit in salted water until tender Cover with you favorite barbecue sauce and grill over charcoal or broil until sauce is hot.

RACOON RECIPES

Baked Racoon

1 small coon or hindquarter and loin of larger young coon 2 to 2 1/2 lbs.
3-4 cups cold water
1 tbsp. Salt
1/3 tsp.black pepper
Salt
Sugar
1 onion
3 stalks celery
3 carrots, diced
2 cloves garlic
1 clove
1 tsp. Sage
1/4 cup vinegar
1 tsp. dark brown sugar

Set oven to moderate hot (400 degrees) 10 minutes before baking. Dress coon carefully so as not to leave any clinging hair. Remove scent glands and kernels under legs.

Wrap coon in plastic wrap or foil and chill thoroughly or freeze for 2 to 3 hours. Trim off all but a thin layer of fat and any discolored spots. Wash well in lukewarm water.

Cut whole coon or hindquarters and loin into 4 pieces with kitchen scissors or heavy butcher knife. Put into 6 qt. kettle, add water to cover, then vegetables, salt, sugar, seasonings, garlic and pepper. Heat to boiling; reduce heat to simmering, cover and cook until tender (1-2 hrs depending on age of animal). Puree vegetables in a blender to thicken sauce.

Bake sweet potatoes or winter squash to go with the dish. A tart vegetable such as sweet-sour red cabbage, or pickled beets are a good accompaniment. Serves 4.

Racoon with Salsa

One Racoon
Salsa to your taste garlic powder

Boil prepared racoon until tender. Cut up meat and cover with a commercial salsa with a little extra garlic; bake at 325 degrees for approx. 30 minutes.

Racoon in Barbecue Sauce

1 small to medium raccoon cut into serving size pieces
1/2 tsp. Salt
1 teaspoon instant minced onion
1 bell pepper
1 1/2 teaspoon Worcestershire sauce
1 (7 oz.) bottle of beer or pickle juice

Place pieces of Beaver or raccoon in a foil-lined roasting pan. Preheat oven to 350 degrees F. and roast, covered for a half hour. After meat has roasted a half hour, uncover and pour barbecue sauce over the pieces. Then roast, uncovered, for another half hour to an hour—until tender. Baste 2 to 3 times during cooking, using your barbecue sauce.

Racoon Patties

Clean and Wash Racoon Thoroughly being careful to take out scent glands under forelegs.

One Racoon
1 cup bread crumbs
1 cup chopped onion
1 egg
Salt and Pepper
Quarter cup bacon fat
1 cup currant Jelly
2 tbsp.frozen orange juice 1 tsp. Garlic powder

Remove meat from bones and grind. Add bread crumbs, onion, garlic, salt, pepper, egg, and fat; mix thoroughly. Form into patties; dip into egg; then dip in bread crumbs. Saute in bacon fat until brown. Cover with currant jelly sauce and place in slow oven for 1 hour.

OPOSSUM RECIPES

Stuffed Opossum

1 raccoon
1 qt. cold water
1/8 cup salt
5 beef bouillon cubes
2 bay leaves
3 celery stalks (chopped)
2 onions (sliced)
1 bag packaged stuffing

Preheat oven to 350 degrees F. Soak raccoon in cold salt water for 10 hours. Rinse meat in cold water and refrigerate 2-4 hours. Prepare stuffing according to package directions and mix with onions and chopped celery.

Stuff raccoon cavity with stuffing. Close cavity tightly. Place stuffed raccoon in roasting pan; add water, bouillon cubes, bay leaves. After 2 hours, turn meat. Reduce heat to 300 degrees F. Cook for 1 more hour.

Test roast; if not done, reduce heat and cook until done.

SQUAB RECIPES

Sautéed Squab and Pears

4 Squabs (about 1 pound each)
1/4 cup Bacon Fat or Olive oil
Salt and pepper to taste
4 Pears, halves
1 cup Port wine

Directions

Marinate pear halves in Port

Split Squabs and brush with bacon fat. Then sprinkle with salt and pepper.

Saute squab in olive oil or bacon fat for 2 minutes each side or until fork tender.

Put on a platter with the marinated pears. Deglaze the pan with Port wine and pour sauce over birds.

Squab Stew

Ingredients

4 squab, cleaned and dressed
6 Medium/Small onions
18 Baby Carrots
1 tbsp. Garlic powder
6 small potatoes
2 tsp. Thyme
2 cups Port Wine
1 cup chopped Celery
2 tsp. Salt
2 tsp. Pepper
2 cups Port wine

Directions

Split Squab into two pieces.

Put all other ingredients in a large pot. Top with Squab pieces. Cover and simmer until Squab is tender.

French Style Squab)

4 Squab
4 tbsp. Olive oil
3 sliced Onions
1 cup of Chicken broth
1 cup sliced mushrooms
1 cup frozen Orange Juice
1 tbsp. Dill
1 tbsp. Cornstarch
1 tsp. MSG

Cut each squab into quarters and Saute in Olive oil for 12-15 minutes.

Remove from pan and keep warm in a serving pot. Saute onions and mushrooms. Add chicken broth, cornstarch and orange juice. Mix with a fork or whisk and bring to boiling point.

Pour orange sauce over Squab and serve.

Broiled Squab

4 Squab
2 tbsp. Olive oil
1 cup orange marmalade
1 tsp. Salt
1 tsp. Pepper
1 can Mandarin Orange sections

Directions

Split Squab and cook under broiler for 15 minutes or till tender.

Drain Can of mandarin oranges and mix with marmelade. Heat and slather over Squab pieces

SQUIRREL RECIPES

Dutch Oven Squirrel

4-6 dressed squirrels, cut in pieces
1/4 cup soy sauce
2 cups water
1/4 cup firmly packed brown sugar
1 small bag baby carrots
1/4 tsp. garlic powder
1/4 tsp. ground ginger
1/4 tsp. Sage one onion
2-3 stalks celery

Add all ingredients to a large pot or Dutch oven. Cover with water and cook on low heat for 3 hours. Remove squirrels. Blend vegetables to thicken gravy. Add squirrels and gravey back to pot. Simmer for 2-3 minutes.

Correct seasonings aand serve.

Crock Pot Squirrel

4-6 dressed Squirrels cut into serving size pieces
1/4 cup soy sauce
1/4 cup water
1/4 cup firmly packed brown sugar
3 tbsp. lemon or lime juice
1/4 tsp. garlic powder
1/4 tsp. ground ginger

Place squirrel halves or Squirrel pieces in crock pot. Mix all ingredients in a small bowl and pour over meat. Cover and cook on low heat for 7-8 hours. To thicken gravy, use either flour or cornstarch mixed with water.

Cook on high until thickened.

Squirrel Pot Pie

2 dressed squirrels (2-2 1/2 lbs.)
2 cups water or chicken stock
2 celery stalks
8 small carrots
1 chopped onion
1 1/2 tsp. Salt
2 tbsp. butter
Dash of black pepper
Rolled dumplings oregano

This is an excellent way to cook old squirrels which are too tough for frying. Wipe thoroughly with a damp cloth and remove all hair. Remove any shot and scent glands. Wash well inside and out with warm water. Cut into serving pieces. Put squirrel into a kettle; add vegetables, oregano, water or stock, salt, pepper and butter; heat to boiling. Reduce heat; cover tightly and simmer until very tender (2-3 hours depending on age of animal). The meat should be almost ready to fall from the bones. Add water as needed.

Remove and blend vegetables on high. Return to pot. Increase the heat until liquid boils. Lay the rolled dumplings over the top of squirrel; cover tightly and cook for 12-15 minutes. Do not lift cover during cooking. Place squirrel in a hot serving dish and arrange dumplings around the edge. Cooking the dumplings in the liquid should thicken the gravy to just the right consistency. Pour gravy over squirrel and dumplings.

Squirrel Stew

2 old squirrels, cut up
2 tbsp. bacon Fat
1 onion, chopped
1 green pepper, chopped
1/4 cup chopped celery
1 clove garlic, chopped
1 cup uncooked rice
1 green pepper, chopped
3 med. potatoes, chopped
Salt and pepper
Water

Brown squirrels in skillet with small amount of fat. Place squirrel in pot and cook until tender. Saute onion, green pepper, celery, and garlic in drippings in skillet; add rice, squirrel, potatoes, seasonings, and enough liquid to cook rice and potatoes.

Cover; simmer slowly until tender.

Squirrel Brunswick Stew

This is the oldest known American Recipefrom Brunswick County in Virginia. The story is that some hunter went out to shoot some game. They left one of the party behind. They came up empty handed but when the returned they found he had caught a squirrel and made a stew. This is the recipe—or at least our version of it.

2-3 squirrels, cut up
3-4 celery stalks
2 onions, chopped
13 small carrots
1 can or three quarters cup corn
1 can stewed tomatoes
1-2 clove garlic, chopped
1 one half cups lima beans
Salt and pepper to taste
2 tsp. thyme
1 tsp. oregano
Water

Brown squirrels and onion in skillet with small amount of fat. Place squirrel in pot with the remaining vegetables and and herbs and simmer until tender. Add liquid as necessary.

We find it best to refrigerate the dish overnight to meld flavors and serve the next day.

However, this is not part of the original Brunswick County Virginia recipe.

Also, today a chicken is substituted for squirrel (or rabbit).

TURTLE RECIPES

Turtle Stew

2 lbs. Turtle meat
4 tbsp. butter
6 celery talks
1 can zucchini in tomato sauce
2 quarts water
1 pkg. fresh mushrooms
2 lg. onions, chopped
1 tsp. Garlic powder
1 cup potatoes, diced
1 tbsp. sugar salt and pepper

Cut Turtle meat into bite-size pieces.

Put it into a pot with 2 quarts boiling water for 20 minutes. Add remaining ingredients except for the potatoes and simmer until the meat is tender.

Add diced potatoes and rest of stock and cook for one half hour more.

Turtle Soup #1

1 med. Turtle 2 lbs. meat)
1 cup onion, chopped
1 green or yellow sweet pepper, diced
3 tbsp. flour
2 hard boiled eggs, sliced
2 tbsp. bacon fat
2 stalkss celery
1/2 tsp. thyme
4 tbsp. tomato paste
1 qt. hot water
1 cup Sherry wine
Salt and pepper to taste
1/2 lemon sliced

Cut Turtle eat into pieces. Saute until brown. Add onion, celery, thyme, green/yelloq pepper, tomato paste, salt, pepper, and flour. Stir well.

Add water and simmer for 1 to 1 1/2 hours. Remove from heat and add wine.

Serve with slices of egg and lemon in each bowl of soup.

Turtle Soup #2

1 med. Turtle 2 lbs. meat)
1 cup onion, chopped
1 can Italian Style tomatoes
2 large can V8
1 can artichoke hearts
2 stalkss chopped celery
1/2 tsp. thyme
1/2 tsp. garlic powder
1 qt. hot water
Salt and pepper to taste

Cut Turtle eat into pieces. Saute until brown. Add onion, celery, bay leaf, thyme, Italian Style tomatoes, salt and pepper, Stir

Add V8 and simmer for 1 to 1 1/2 hours adding more water as needed. Remove from heat and add wine.

Serve with an artichoke heart and slices of egg in each bowl of soup.

Barbecued Turtle

One pound Turtle meat cut into chunks and cooked in water, celery, salt and pepper and onions until tender. Discard vegetables.

Place the Turtle in a baking dish and add your favorite barbecue sauce.

Cook in a 250 degree oven for 20-30 minutes until suace gets hot. Add a liberal amount of sherry and serve.

Turtle (terrapin) Newburg

1/2 lb. tender Turtle meat simmered in celery, onion, salt & pepper
2 cups of milk
1 pkg. White or Bechamel sauce
2 celery stalk and one small onion boiled tender salt and pepper to taste
1/2 tsp. garlic powder
1/2 tsp. chili powder
1 tsp. Paprika
2 tbsp. sherry wine

Simmer Turtle with Celery, Onion salt and pepper until tender.

Use all other ingredients to make Newburg sauce

Combine all ingredients and serve hot

1/2 lb. tender Turtle meat simmered in celery, onion, salt & pepper
2 cups of milk
1 pkg. White or Bechamel sauce
2 celery stalk and one small onion boiled tender
salt and pepper to taste
1/2 tsp. garlic powder
1/2 tsp. chili powder
1 tsp. Paprika
2 tbsp. sherry wine

Simmer Turtle with Celery, Onion salt and pepper until tender.

Use all other ingredients to make Newburg sauce*

Combine all ingredients and serve hot

Note: Canned terrapin can be used.

Fried Soft Shell Turtle

2 lbs. Turtle meat, cut into 2-4 inch pieces
1/2 cup Port Wine
1 tsp. salt
1/2 cup all-purpose flour
1/4 cup plus
1 tbsp. milk
2 eggs, separated
1 tbsp. Bacon fat
1/8 tsp. salt
I pt. Wesson oil

Combine Turtle, Port wine, and 1 tsp. salt. Cover with water; simmer 1 hour or until tender. Drain and set aside.

Combine flour, milk, egg yolks, olive oil, and 1/8 tsp. salt; mix well. Beat egg whites until stiff; fold into batter.

Dip Turtle pieces into batter; fry until golden brown in deep oil heated to 375 degrees F. Drain well on paper towels. Yield: 4-6 servings.

VENISON RECIPES

Barbecued Venison Ribs

1 Quart Buttermilk
6 lb. Venison ribs with some loin meat attached
Red Wine sufficient to cove ribs in a marinade 1 1/2 c Water
1 cup Currant or plum jelly or jam
1/2 Brown sugar
1/4 md Onions, finely diced
1/8 tsp.cloves
1/2 tsp.dry mustard 1/2 tsp. garlic powder 1/2 ts Salt
Black pepper and salt to taste

Marinate Ribs in buttermilk for two hours with 1 tsp. Meat tenderizer. Then wash off buttertmilk
Preheat oven to 325 degrees. Combine all ingredients except the ribs in a large bowl. Blend well and sprinkle ribs with pepper and additional salt.

Place in 5 qt. roasting pan in double layer. Roast 1 hour.

Pour sauce over ribs. Increase heat to 350 degrees and bake until ribs just begin to char on top, about 1 1/2 hours. Turn ribs over cover pan and bake about 30 minutes longer, until ribs are tender and sauce is thick (If necessary, add water). To serve, place ribs on serving platter. Pour sauce over ribs. Makes about 6 servings. >

Barbecued Venison Chops

20 venison chops
6 oz Beer
1 large. Onion, chopped and sauteed
4 pats of butter
2 oz Garlic Salt

Place aluminum foil on hot grill with sides folded up, so there is no runoff of juices. Place chops on foil. Add beer, sauteed onion and butter. Sprinkle garlic salt on chops each time you turn them. Do not cook chops. When they are warm, remove foil from grill.

Venison Curry

2 lbs. Venison roast, steak of filet marinated till tender in buttermilk and tenderizer
1 can golden mushroom soup
1 soup can water
1 med. bell pepper, chopped
1 large onion, chopped
1 tbsp. Curry powder or to taste
2 tbsp. Bacon fat
1 tsp. Chili powder
Salt and pepper
1 tsp. MSG

Cut venison into bite-size chunks and salt and pepper to taste; then roll in flour to coat.

Put Mushroom Soup, water, bell pepper and onions in a pot and simmer until tender. Add water if necessary.

Add Venison and seasonings to pot. Simmer until venision is warm (2 minutes) stirring to mix thoroughly. Serve immediately with Chutney and Rice. Do NOT overcook.

Quick Cooked Venison

1-2 lbs. cubed venison, marinated in buttermilkwith tenderizer, then washed and cleaned
4-6 baby carrots
1-2 med. onion, chopped
1 diced celery stalk
2 ounces butter
1-2 tbsp. bacon fat
1/4-1/2 tsp. sage
1 tsp. Sugar
Flour to thicken
1 cup sherry or red wine

Barely Brown venison in butter. Add seasonings, celery, carrots, onion, carrots, and enough wine and water to cover meat. Cook until tender; thicken sauce with flour and add wine. Good with white or wild rice.

Venison Tenderloin

1 venison tenderloin
2 tbsp. Bacon fat
1 tsp. black pepper
1 can Peaches
1 can Apricots
6 dried apricots
1 tbsp. Sugar
1/2 tsp. MSG
Preheat oven to 170 F.

Drain cans of Apricot and Peaches. Add dried Apricots and put fruit in a blender and blend on high. Add 1 tbsp. sugar and 1/2 tsp. MSG. Warm sauce.

Put Venison in a pan. Cover with Bacon Fat and sprinkle with Salt and Pepper.

Place in the oven. Remove venison as soon as it is warm. Do NOT overcook' Cut into slices and cover with fruit sauce and serve.

Venison Tid Bits

2 lbs. Venison
1 tsp. thyme
One half tsp. tarragon
1/2 tsp. garlic powder
1 cup. diced onions
1 cup sliced mushrooms
4 oz. Bacon Fat
Salt and pepper to taste
Buttermilk
Venison Saute

Cut venison into bite-size chunks. Then, marinate the venison for 3 hours in buttermilk. If it is an old animal add a little tenderizer. Wash venison thoroughly to remove buttermilk.

Heat oven to 170 F. Use 2 oz of bacon fat to coat the venison pieces.

Then heat in oven until the venison is warm.

Lightly saute the onion, mushrooms, thyme and garlic powder in the remaining bacon fat.

Slice the venison on a warm serving dish, top with sauteed onion/ mushroom mix and serve.

Venison Sauteed

2-3 lbs. Venison
1/2 cup olive oil
1/4 tsp. black pepper
1/3 cup Port Wine
3/4 tsp. Salt
1 large onion, chopped
1/4 tsp. garlic salt (or to taste)
1 tsp. sugar
1 tsp. oregano

Marinate the Venison in buttermilk or yogurt for 3 hours to clean the taste. If meat is tough, add tenderizer. Then wash thoroughly.

Reserve ½ the oil foe sauteing. Then mix all ingredients together and remarinate the Venison for 3 hours to flavor it.

Saute the venison quickly and very lightly. Sprinkle pepper. Slice and serve. If you like, boil down the wine marinade for a sauce oe serve with your favorit meat or barbecue sauce. Great for sandwiches.

Venison Cassoulet

(This is longer than our usual Recipes but it will feed and army and can be frozen)

2-3 lbs. Cubed venison
I package Great Northern Beans
1 med. onion, diced
6-8 baby carrots
2 stalks celery, diced
3 tbsp. tomato paste
1 Quart stock
Salt and pepper
Garlic to taste
One half tsp. Thyme
One half tsp.Tarragon
One half tsp. Oregano
1 tbsp. Sugar
One Kielb.asa skinned and diced

Marinate venison cubes in buttermilk wit one tsp. meat tenderizer
Soak beans in water overnight,

Drain Beans. Add all other ingredients to pot and simmer until tender.

Simmer until venison is tender. Correct seasonings and serve.

Venison Pepper Steak

2 lbs. sliced meat marinated in bruuermilk then washed clean
Flour for dredging meat
Salt and ground red & black pepper to taste
2 medium chopped onion
1 box sliced mushrooms
2 tbsp. Bacon Fat
1 cup Port wine
1 tsp. Garlic powder

Coat meat with flour after it has been salted and peppered and seasones.

Warm quickly in low heat Bacon Fat. Cook covered until meat is pink in the center.

Remove meat from pan and make gravy by adding deglazing residue with Port wine and pour wine sauce over steaks.

Cook onion and muchrooms together separately and serve with the meat

Venison Cassoulet

Chefs Note: This is longer than our usual Recipes but just as easy and it is delicious, easy to make and will feed an army

2 lb. Cubed venison
1 package Great Northern Beans
1 med. onion, diced
6 small carrots
2 stalks celery, diced
3 tbsp. tomato paste
1 Quart stock
Salt and pepper
Garlic to taste
One half tsp. Thyme
One half tsp.Tarragon
One half tsp. Oregano one Kielb.asa skinned and diced
2 tbsp. MSG

Marinate venison cubes in buttermilk with one tsp. meat tenderizer overnight.

Soak beans in water overnight,

Drain Beans. Wash milk off venisonAdd all ingredients to pot and simmer until tender.

Simmer until venison is tender. Add water as necessary to prevent sticking to bottom of pan. Correct seasonings and serve.

Venison Pepper Steak

2 lbs. sliced meat marinated in buttermilk then washed clean
Flour for dredging meat
Salt and ground Chili powswe to taste
2 medium chopped onion
1 box sliced mushrooms

Coat meat with flour after it has been salted and peppered. Brown outside quickly in moderately hot cooking oil. Remove meat from pan.

Saute onions and muchrooms together, separately fro meat and serve with the meat. Reserve and keep warm. Then make gravy by adding de glazing the pan with red wine or sherry.

Venison Enchiladas

1 lb. ground venison
1 onion
Olive oil or bacon fat salt and pepper
1 tsp. garlic powder
1 tbsp. sugar
2 cans enchilada sauce
1 dozen corn tortillas
1/2 lb. sharp cheddar cheese, grated
6 black olives, chopped

Place venison and onion in skillet and saute in oil until meat is browned and onion cooked through. Stir in garlic, sugar, olives and salt and pepper to taste. Heat enchilada sauce in large round pan. Dip each tortilla in the hot sauce, remove almost at once and place on flat surface.

Spoon 1 tablespoon of meat mixture on tortilla, roll up, and place in greased 9x13 baking dish. Repeat with all tortillas and make single layer in dish, top with cheese.

Bake 15-20 minutes at 375 degrees F.

Baked Venison Steak

1 lb. Venison round steak sliced and marinated in Buttermilk and tenderizer then washed clean
1 tsp. Salt
1 diced onion
1 tsp. pPepper
One half box sliced musrooms
1 tbsp. flour
1 minced garlic clove
1 green bell pepper
1 tbsp. bacon fat or olive oil
1 cup red wine of sherry

Salt and pepper 8-10 pieces of venison steak and roll in flour. Place in baking container and saute in hot oil until brown. Add all other ingredients and stir. Bake in 300 oven for 45 minutes. Add water as needed. Correct seasonings.

Grilled Venison Steak

Marinate 4 (1/2" thick) venison steaks in buttermilk and meat tenderizer for 24 hours. Then wash thoroughly.
Enough dry Mustard to coat meat
1 tbsp. pepper
2 tbsp. olive oil
1/4 cup margarine
Dash salt

This only works on an outdoor grill. Brush venison steaks (from leg, rib, or loin chops of young animal) with olive oil. Coat the Steaks with dry mustard and pepper. Grill the steaks until done to taste. Combine margarine and salt and brush on broiled steaks.

Stuffed Venison Steak

1 lb. round venison steak cut thin
1/2 tsp. Each Salt and Pepper
1/2 tsp. Garlic powder
1 egg
1/2 cup milk or broth
1 medium diced onion
1 cup Stuffing Mix
1 tbsp. flour
1/2 cup sherry
2 tbsp. bacon fat

Marinate round steak in buttermilk and tenderizer

Mix bread crumbs, milk, sherry, egg, and seasonings to make stuffing.

Salt the meat and cut into 2" x 4" pieces. Spread each piece or meat with dressing and roll, fastening the rolls with toothpicks. Roll in flour and brown in fat. Place in pan, add, cover and cook for 1 hr. at 300 degrees.

Venison Steak au Poire

Cut steaks thin and marinate Steaks in Buttermilk AND tenderizer.
2 lbs. venison steak
2 tbsp. Olive oil
Salt and fresh ground pepper garlic powder to taste
1 cup sour cream
2 tbsp. sherry

Wash steaks thoroughly, Sprinkle salt and cover with pepper steaks and saute in olive oil. When nicely brown, remove from pan and reserve. Add garlic and sherry to deglaze pan. Add sour cream over cutlets and stir to make a sauce.

Pour sauce over steaks and serve. Serves 6-8.

If you do NOT add tenderizer, simply warm steaks. Do NOT cook

Sauteed Filet of Venison

Wash venison thoroughly.
Cut filet into 3/4" to 1" thick slices butter
Frozen lemonade (easier)

Brush sliced fillet with a very small amount of lemonade. let standfo 115 minutes. If using lemon slices, alternate the slices of venison and lemon, put in refrigerator; wait 15-30 minutes. Remove, turn over, and rebrush with lemonad. Again, let stand in refrigerator 15-30 minutes.

Warm filets in skillet but do NOT cook. Turn cook until rare. Sprinkle with salt and serve. Serve rare. Do not overcook as venison is dry and will toughen almost immediately.

Easy Barbecued Venison

2 lbs. venison
Your favorite barbecue sauce
1 tsp. Garlic Powder
1 quart venison or beef stock
1/2 cup port wine

Mix Garlic powder and port wine into barbecue Sauce
Cook venison in stock until well done. Cool. Remove meat from bones and cut up. Save and freeze Stock!

Put meat on a serving dish. Pour barbecue sauce mix over meat and put in oven to heat. This is a good way to use the bony parts of a deer.

Venison Strogonoff

2 lbs. Venison roast, steak of filet marinated in buttermilk and tenderizer
4 tbsp. Bacon fat
1 large onion, chopped
Flour to coat meat
Salt and pepper
One half pt. sour cream
One cup bechamel (White) sauce*
1 tsp. garlic powder
4 tbsp. Flour
1 tsp. MSG

Mix butter and flour in a double boiler. Slowly ad milk and seasonings, stirring to blend

Cut venison into bite-size chunks, salt and pepper to taste, roll in flour to coat. Heat bacon fat to hot, saute venison quickly, remove from pan.

Add pepper and onions and cook until tender. Drain off bacon fat. Add sour cream. Return venison to pan. Stir to mix thoroughly; cover with a lid and simmer until tender. Serve over rice.

Venison Roast

4 lb. Venison Round
4-6 slices of bacon
1 tsp. Salt
One half tsp. pepper
1 quart meat stock
2 tsp. garlic powder six small carrots
1 pkg mushrooms
1 medium onion one half cup minced celery
1 cup Port wine

Saute 6 slices of bacon (crisp) in Dutch oven. Remove bacon and leave grease in oven. Sprinkle roast with garlic powder, salt and pepper. Heat bacon grease and sear roast on all sides until brown. Add diced diced onion, carrots, mushrooms and celery. Cook very slowly for about 3 hours (or until done). Blend vegetables to thicken sauce. Add Port Wine and serve.

Venison Steaks in Sherry Sauce

4 venison T-bone or loin steaks, cut about 1/2 inch thick
1/2 cup sherry
3 Tbsp. butter salt and pepper
1 tbsp. chopped chives
2 tbsp. Blackberry or currant jelly
1/8 tsp.nutmeg
1 tsp. sugar

Trim any excess fat from steaks. Sprinkle steaks with salt, pepper and sugar then saute steaks in a 10-inch pan over medium heat, in warm butter—about 1 or 2 minutes on each side until warm.

Remove from heat and place on warm platter.

Pour off fat. Deglaze pan with sherry. Mix with nutmeg, chives and Blackberry jelly/jam. Pour sauce over steaks and serve.

Venison Soup

Venison Soup

1 1/2 pounds venison diced into 1/2-3/4 inch pieces
2 quarts water
1 quart can Chicken stock
I large diced onion.
12 baby carrots
1 cup chopped celery
Salt to taste
2 tsp. Chili Powder
1 tbsp. Sugar
2 tbsp. Bacon fat
1 can sweet corn
1 tsp. Garlic powder
2 tsp. MSG

In a big pot, saute onions until brown. Drain the corn and add the remainder of ingredients. Cover with water and stock. Simmer on low for two hours or until meat is tender.

Correct the seasonings and serve. You can either freeze the soup or store it in the frig.

Easy Venison Soup

1 1/2 pound venison cut into 1/2-3/4 inch pieces.
1 pkg. Onion soup mix
1 cans golden mushroom soup
1 tbsp. Frozen orange juice
1 tsp. msg
1 can Italian style stewed tomatoes
1 tbsp. Chili Powder

Saute venison until brown in the bottom of your pot. Add remaining ingredients with water and simmer until tender. Add water as needed. Correct seasonings and serve.

Venison Vegetable Pot

Neck or backbone broken in chunks, fat removed
1 chopped onion
1 tsp. garlic powder
2 cups meat stock
2 tsp. salt
1 tsp. Chile Powder
One half cup all purpose flour
10 baby carrots
1 cup lima beans
1 can corn drained
2 med. potatoes cooked and diced
1/2 cup all purpose flour
One half cup brandy or sherry
1/2 cup cream
3 ribs of celery, chopped salt and pepper to taste

Thoroughly clean and wash venison. Place venison, stock, onion, garlic, carrots, celery, salt and pepper in pot; cover and boil. Reduce heat and simmer for 2 hours. Add water as needed. Remove bones from pot, pick meat, and dice.

Strain some broth and blender with flour. Add to pot with cream, potatoes, corn and lima beans. Correct seasonings, add brandy or sherry, cover and bake at 350 degrees for 20 minutes and serve.

Strain some broth and blender with flour. Add to pot with cream, potatoes, corn and lima beans. Correct seasonings, add brandy or sherry, cover and bake at 350 degrees for 20 minutes and serve.

Venison Crown Roast

1 rack of venison
Salt pork for larding
Freshly ground black pepper
4 to 5 tbsp. butter, melted

It is easy to prepare the meat. The backbone must be cut with a saw between each rib portion enough so the ribs can be bent and then tied into a crown,

The rib bones are left rather long so they curve dramatically outwardly as the meat section is turned to the center. You then want to remove the fat and place bacon over the chops.

Preheat oven to 450 F. Place in roasting pan, coat with the butter and sprinkle with pepper. Roast for 15 minutes. Lower heat to 350 F. and continue to roast 12 to 15 minutes per pound—NO LONGER. Baste occasionally.

While the venison is roasting begin to prepare a Cumberland Sauce. There is an excellent on in the Joy of Cooking or you can use this as well. Mix:

1-1/2 cups red wine
1 half cup brown sugar
1 quarter tsp. cloves
1 quarter tsp. ginger
1 quarter tsp. Pepper
1 cup Currant of Blackberry Jelly
1 tsp. thyme
Salt

Venison Stock

Thoroughly clean and wash venison
Venison
Water to cover
2 Large chopped Onions
Garlic Powder
Salt and Pepper
2 tsp. sugar
1 tsp. MSG
2 tbsp. butter or bacon fat

Marinate venison in buttermilk and themn wash to remove gamey taste.

Cut off all fat. Boil meat, onions and seasonings in water to cover until it falls off bone;.

Remove meat and cut it into small pieces. Put in frying pan with butter or bacon fat and saute until slightly brown. Correct all seasonings. Save the meat for hash. Use the stock for gravies or freeze.

Ginger Venison

2 lbs. cubed venison roast or steak
2 chopped onions
1 1/2 tsp. salt
1 tsp. Chili Powder
1 can stewed Italian tomatoes
1 tsp. turmeric
1 tsp. cumin
1/2 cup oil
1 tbsp. sugar
2 tsp. Garlic Powder
4 tsp. powdered ginger
1 can onion soup

Combine onions, turmeric, ginger, salt, and meat. Let stand 1 hour. Saute lightly in large frying pan. Add tomatoes, seasonings and onion soup; cover and simmer 1 1/2 hours adding water (or Port wine) if the mixture gets too dry. Serve over rice.

Venison Roast in Sour Cream

3 lbs. venison roast. Then marinate overnight in buttermilk with meat tenderizer if this is an old animal and wash thoroughly
3 tbsp. olive oil or bacon fat
1 pint sour cream
1 Quart meat stock
2 onions diced
Garlic Powder to taste
1 tsp. Powdered sage, 2 tsp. Leaf sage
1 tsp. Each Chili Powder and Salt
1 tsp. Each of Chili Powder and Salt
1/2 tsp. MSG

Brown the roast and the onions in the pot. Add stock and seasonings and roast till tender. At the end, add the sour cream but so not boil.

Venison Roast in Sherry

Wash one venison roast thoroughly
One pkg. dry onion soup mix
I tsp. garlic
1 cup sherry wine
1 tbsp. sugar

Preheat oven to 425 degrees then reduce the heat to 350 degrees. Place roast on a large piece of heavy duty aluminum foil. Sprinkle 1/2 pkg. of dry onion soup over meat. Wrap the venison in the foil and seal the edges tightly.

Place the wrapped meat in a baking pan and roast for 2 to 2 1/2 hours or until tender. Remove the roast and put it on a pleat. Pour off any fat from the juices. Add red wine sage, sugar and juices and thicken with flour or corn starch to make a gravy. (Tip: use corn starch if you want a lighter gravy

Venison Roast in Sherry

Wash one venison roast thoroughly
1 2-4 LB. Venison Roast
One pkg. dry onion soup mix
I tsp. garlic
1 tsp. Chili Powder
2 tsp. Sage
1 cup sherry wine
1 tbsp. sugar

Preheat the oven to 350 degrees. Place roast on a large piece of heavy duty aluminum foil. Sprinkle Chili Powder, Sage and 1/2 pkg. of dry onion soup over meat. Wrap the venison in the foil and seal the edges tightly.

Place the wrapped meat in a baking pan and roast for 2 to 2 1/2 hours or until tender. Remove the roast and put it on a pleat. Pour off any fat from the juices. Add the Sherry wine sage, sugar and juices and thicken with flour or corn starch to make a gravy. (Tip: use corn starch if you want a lighter gravy

Mexican Venison Stew

Serves 5
3 lbs. Venison, cut into 1" cubes
1 pound bite size Chirozo sausages
2 cans red beans
1 large can tomatoes
3 medium onions, diced 1"
15 Baby Carrots
3 stalks celery, diced 1"
2 tsp. Garlic Powder
1 pkg. sliced mushrooms
2 tbsp. chili powder
2 cups red wine
2 cups meat stock
1 teaspoon salt
1/2 tsp. ground thyme
2 large green peppers, seeded and diced

Brown venison and sausage in a large pot, add all vegetable except beans and sauté for 5 more minutes. Then add the beef stock and cook for 3 minutes. Then add red wine and seasonings.

Let simmer 1 hour and serve with hot French bread. IMPORTANT—stir occasiionally so the stew does not stick to the bottom of the pot and burn. At the end Blend vegetables on high to thicken sauce. Add the Beans and simmer 3 minutes longer. Serves 10.

Elegant Venison Stew

2 lbs. Venison steak
1/2 lb. Bacon or salt pork
2 tbsp. flour
2 cups of stock
1 can Italian stewed tomatoes or preferably zucchini
8 baby carrots
2 Stalks diced celery diced
1 tbsp. sugar
7 small onions
Garlic Powder to taste
1 cup peas
Salt and pepper to taste
4 cups Port wine

Cut bacon into 1" cubes and saute in large saucepan until lightly browned.

Remove and set aside. Cut venison into 1 1/2 or 2" pieces and brown over high heat in bacon fat. Stir in flour and make a roux. Lower heat and let brown 2-3 minutes. Then add stock and stir till smooth. Simmer 1 hour or more until venison begins to get tender, add more liquid as necessary.

Add all the other ingredients, except peas, and continue to simmer to make a thick stew. Simmer peas in a separate pan until done. Strain and spoon over or around stew when served. Serve with corn muffins, potatoes or parsnips and a salad.

Irish Venison Stew

Cut venison into chunks and marinate venison in buttermilk to clean taste and tenderize the meat.

2 pounds of your a chosen, (Venison, Buffalo, Elk, Beef, Antleope, Lamb)
1 tsp. Dry M ustard
1 tablespoon black peppercorns
3 garlic cloves, coarsely chopped
1-1/2 cups Port wine
2 to 3 tbsp. olive oil
2 cups celery, cut into 1-inch diagonals
6 to 8 peeled small boiling onions
1-2 cups beef stock salt and pepper to tasrw
1/2 cup freshly hand picked shamrocks (for garnish)

Wash buttermilk off the venison. Mix the meat, juniper berries, peppercorns and garlic. Add 1 cup of the red wine. Cover and marinate in the refrigerator for 2 to 3 hours, or overnight.

Drain off the marinade and save. Heat the olive oil in your pot and brown the venison. Add the celery and onions. Add all the red wine and 3/4 cup beef stock. Cover and bake in a preheated 350°F oven for 45 minutes, or until tender, adding the remaining beef stock during baking if necessary.

Remove from the oven. Season with salt and pepper and serve. Garnish serving platc with shamrocks and have a happy St. Patrick's day!

Italian Venison Stew

Marinate venison in yogurt or buttermilk. Then wash thoroughly

2 lbs. stew meat
1 can Zucchini
1 cup chopped celery
2 tbsp. olive oil or bacon fat
1 diced medium onion
2 tsp. Garlic powder
1 tsp. salt
1 tbsp. Sugar
1/2 tsp. Pepper
2 cups Port wine
2 tsp. Powdered Oregano or 4 tsp. leaves

Brown the cubed meat in the oil, add two cups of water, then the rest of the ingredients. Cover and simmer 1 1/2 hours. Remove bay leaves, add carrots and potatoes, cook another 30-45 minutes or until tender. As a footnote, I've just browned the meat, then dumped everything in the "crockpot" on low. It produces a stew that tastes as tho' it already been reheated 2 to 3 times.

Basic Venison Stew

Marinate venison in yogurt or buttermilk. Then wash thoroughly

2 lbs. stew meat
12 baby carrots
6 potatoes
2 tbsp. Oil or Bacon Fat
1 tsp. Worcestershire sauce
1 md onion
1 tsp. salt
2 tsp. Sugar
1/2 tsp. Pepper
1 tsp. Garlic powder
1 1/2 tsp. sage
3 cups Port Wine

Brown the cubed meat in the oil, add wine, then the rest of the ingredients.

Cover and simmer 1 1/2 hours. Add carrots and potatoes, cook another 30-45 minutes or until tender.

Check frequently to correct seasonings and add more water or wine as needed.

If you have a crockpot, use that to simmer. Check fluids, correct seasoning and serve.

Venison Stew with Rosemary

3 lbs. boneless venison cut into bite sized portions
1 tbsp. sugar
2 large diced onions
Flour
1 tsp. garlic powder
Salt and pepper to taste
3 tbsp. bacon fat
2 tsp. Rosemary
2 cups meat stock

Marinate venison in buttermilk or yogurt overnight to soften meat and clean taste. Wash thoroughly, dust with flour, salt, and pepper. Brown meat on all sides in bacon fat over medium heat; add onions and remaining ingredients. Cover and simmer approximately 1 1/4 hours or until tender.

Venison Sausage

Mexican Venison Sausage

5 lbs. venison, coarse ground
1 lb. Bacon fat
2 tbsp. monosodium glutamate
1 tsp. jalapeno pepper
2 tbsp. salt
2 tbsp. Sugar
2 large onions processed to liquid
3 green peppers
2 tbsp. Chili Powder
1 tbsp. ground sage
1 tbsp. garlic powder

Grind or process meat, onion and bacon fat. Mix seasonings thoroughly with venison and re-grind or reprocess. Cook a small sample to test flavor.

Adapt spices to taste. Wine may be used to moisten the mixture if it is to be stuffed in casings. Keeps well about 1 year in freezer.

Smoked Venison Sausage

4 lbs. meat, 1/2 venison, 1/2 pork
1 cup Bacon Fat
1 tbsp. garlic powder
1 large onion cut fine
1/2 cup salt
1 1/2 tbsp. Chili Powder
3 tbsp. ground sage
1 cup Hickory Flavored Barbecue sauce
1 cup sugar
1 tsp. MSG
1 cup oatmeal (for binder)
1/2 cup water

Clean, wash and grind your venison. Then mix with herbs, salt, msg, Chili Powder, sugar, water, Barbecue Sauce, oatmeal and water.

Mix thoroughly in a food processor. Pack meat in containers sausage casings. The meat may be stored in a freezer and used as you would good pork sausage.

Classic Venison Sausage

2 pounds ground venison from tough cuts like shoulder, flank, or neck
1 pound pork loin and/or shoulder
1 1/2 cups bacon fat
3 tbsp. salt
1 tablespoon ground black pepper
2 tbsp. powdered garlic
1 tbsp. powdered onion
1 tbsp. ground sage, thyme or other favorite seasonings
3 tbsp. ground sage
5-9 tbsp. sugar
4 tbsp. instant oatmeal
1 tbsp. msg. (accent)

Grind The Venison and Pork together

Add all ingredients and mix well. Add water if mix is too dry. Freeze the mix in plastic containers. Unfreeze, make into portion size pieces and saute and serve needed. Refreeze the rest of the sausage to use on the next occasion.

Spicey Venison Sausage

5 lbs. venison, coarse ground
2 cups bacon fat
1 tbsp. monosodium glutamate
1 tsp. jalapeno pepper
3 tbsp. salt
3 tbsp. sugar
2 tbsp. garlic powder
3 red bell peppers
3 tbsp. Chili Powder
Red wine
1 tbsp. ground sage

Process ground venison and bacon fat together. Spread on a clean surface and sprinkle evenly with seasonings, mix thoroughly and re-grind if necessary. Test hotness by sauteing a small sample. Adjust seasonings. If the mix is too mild add seasonings. If too salty or too hot add more meat.

Wine may be used to moisten the mixture. Store in containers covering the meat with plastic wrap to avoid dehydration.

Keeps well about 1 year in freezer.

Italian Venison Sausage

4 lbs. venison, coarse ground
12 ounces bacon fat
1 tbsp. monosodium glutamate
2 tbsp. ground Oregano
3 tbsp. salt
5 tbsp. black pepper
5 tbsp. sugar
2 tbsp. garlic powder
2 finely chopped onions
3 tbsp. Parmesan cheece

Process ground venison and bacon fat together. Spread on a clean surface and sprinkle evenly with seasonings, mix thoroughly and re-grind if necessary.

Test hotness by sauteing a small sample. Adjust seasonings. If the mix is too mild add seasonings. If too salty or too hot add more meat. Wine may be used to moisten the mixture. Store in containers covering the meat with plastic wrap to avoid dehydration.

Keeps well about 1 year when frozen.

Herbed Venison Sausage

5 lbs. venison, coarse ground
2 cups bacon fat
1 tbsp. monosodium glutamate
2 tbsp. Ground Cinnamon
1 tbsp. Ground Nutmeg
3 tbsp. Salt
1/2 tsp. Ground clovest
1 1/2 tbsp. Chili Powder
5 tbsp. sugar
2 tbsp. garlic powder
3 finely chopped green bell peppers
1 tbsp. MSG

Process ground venison and bacon fat together. Spread on a clean surface and sprinkle evenly with seasonings, mix thoroughly and re-grind if necessary. Test hotness by sauteing a small sample. Adjust seasonings. If the mix is too mild add seasonings. If too salty or too hot add more meat.

Wine may be used to moisten the mixture. Store in containers covering the meat with plastic wrap to avoid dehydration.
Keeps well about 1 year in freezer.

TexMex Venison Sausage

3 lbs. venison, Hamburger
2 lbs. Pork Hamburger
1 Pint Bacon Fat
1 cup smoke flavored Barbecue Sauce
3 tbsp. Chili Powder
3 tbsp. Paprika
1 1/2 tbsp. garlic powder
1 tsp. crushed Jalapeno pepper, to taste
1/4 cup salt
1/4 cup Sugar

Mix all ingredients and grind 2 to 3 times. sausage may be frozen without smoking in patties, sausage bags, or casings.

Sweet Venison Sausage

5 lbs. Ground Venison
2 tbsp. MSG
6 tbsp. sugar
1 1/2 tbsp. black pepper
1 tbsp.Allspice
1 1/2 tbsp. garlic powder
1 tbsp. coriander
1/4 cup salt

Mix all ingredients and gtind 2 to 3 times diced venison. This sausage may be frozen without smoking and made in patties, hors d'oeuvre balls sausage bags, or put into casings.

Miscellaneous Venison Recipes

Venison Cornmeal Meatloaf

1 1/2 lb. Ground Venison
2/3 cup corn meal
1 1/2 cup water
1 tbsp. Flour
2 tsp. Garlic
2 tbsp. bacon fat
1 small chopped onion
2 tsp. Salt
1 tsp. Chili Powder
1 tbsp. sugar
2 eggs

Mix cornmeal, eggs and water in bowl. Brown venison and onion in bacon fat;

Add salt, chili and garlic powder, and cornmeal mixture. Stir continuallyl and cook 15 minutes. Place in greased loaf pan and bake 35-40 minutes at 350 degrees.

Serve Plain or with your favorite Pasta Sauce.

Venison Meatloaf

2 lbs. ground venison
1/2 lb. ground beef
3 tbsp. butter or margarine
1 cup minced onion
1/4 cup minced celery
2 eggs
1 cup quick oatmeal
1/2 cup sherry, red wine or milk
1 tbsp. Each salt and pepper
1 tbsp. sugar
2 tsp. garlic powder
2 tsp. Powdered Thyme leaves
1 tsp. Cinamon leaves

Preaheat oven to 350 degrees. Saute onions and celery until tender, about 5 minutes. Mix oatmeal, eggs, and then all other ingredients except meat in a large bowl. Add venison, beef and onion mixture; mix again.

Place mixture in 9x5" loaf pan and bake 1 1/2 hours. Pour off pan juices. Serve hot or cold with your favorite pasta sauce. Makes 2 to 3 servings.

Venison and Bacon Meatloaf

2 pounds ground venison
One cup ground pork
1 cup minced onion
1 cup bacon fat
1/2 cup minced onion
1/4 cup minced celery
2 eggs
1 cup fresh bread crumbs
1/2 cup milk
2 tsp. Each salt and pepper
1 tsp. thyme leaves
2 tbsp. sugar
3 Bacon slices
1 tsp. Garlic Powder

Preaheat oven to 350 degrees. Beat eggs with a fork. Thoroughly mix eggs and all other ingredients together in a large bowl. Place mixture in loaf pan or pans cover tops with sliced bacon.

Bake 1 hours. Pour off pan juices. Cover with you favorite heated spaghetti sauce and serve.

Venison Hash

3 tbsp. Bacon drippings
1 large Onion, chopped
3 cups Cooked and ground Venison leftovers.
2 Med. potatoes cut in 16 pcs.
1 tbsp. Flour
1 clove minced Garlic
2 cups Beef broth
1/4 tsp. Black pepper
2 tsp. salt
1/4 tsp. thyme
2 tsp. Chili powder

Brown onion and potatoes in bacon fat. Remove vegetables, add flour and mix with fat to make a roux. Replace veggies in pan, add venison, broth and other ingredients. Let simmer until tender.

Venison Sloppy Joe's Mix

2 lbs. venison hamburger
1 cups of chopped onion
1/2 cup bacon fat
1 1/2 cups Pasta Sauce (your Choice)
1 cups water
1 tbsp. Garlic powder
1 tsp. Salt
1 cup chopped green pepper
1 tbsp. Sugar
2 tsp. Chili Powder

Saute onions and venison brown in bacon fat. Add all other ingredients; mix thoroughly; bring to a boil and simmer 5 minutes. Pour into sterile clean Mason pint jars almost to the top. Put on the lids and freeze (safest) or boil the jars again completely covered by water fo 15 minutes. DO NOT OPEN JARS IF THE CENTER OF THE LIDS HAS POPPED UP! THROW AWAY!

Venison with Pasta Roni

3 lbs. ground venison
1 cup chopped onion
1 tsp. Garlic powder
1/4 cup salad oil
2 jars of Pasta sauce
1/2 tsp. pepper
2 tsp. salt for sauce
2 tsp. oregano
2 tbsp. salt for macaroni
1 lb. macaroni product
2 cups cottage cheese
1 lb. Mozzarella cheese, sliced thin
1/2 cup grated Parmesan cheese

This is a good berlly stuffer. Lightly saute ground venison and onion until meat is evenly browned. Add spaghetti sauce and spices. Simmer, stirring occasionally, about 10-15 minutes. Do not allow the sauce to dry out and stick bottom of the pot.

Cook macaroni in salted water, Drain and add cottage cheese. Layer 1/3 of the meat sauce on the bottom of a baking pan. Then add half the macaroni and cheese mix. The another layer of meat and more of the macaroni cheexze mix and a final layer meat.

Cover the top with a thin layer of parmesan cheese. Arrange black olives or canned artichoke hearts on top to decorate and bake at 350 degrees F. 20-30 minutes until bubbly. Cut into serving size pieces and serve with a spatula.

Venison Meat Balls

1 and one half lbs. ground venison
1 cup cooked quick oat meal
1 tsp. Each salt and pepper
2/3 cup onion, finely chopped
One half tsp. sage
Garlic powder (to taste)
1/4 cup bacon fat
1 tbsp. flour
1 cup milk
1/4 tsp. cinnamon, ginger and nutmeg
1 tsp. sugar

Combine oatmeal, venison, salt, pepper, onion, sage and garlic powder; shape into balls about 1" in diameter. Brown meatballs in bacon fat, cover pan; cook over low heat 15 minutes. Remove meatballs from pan and add flour to drippings. Add milk, sugar, cinnamon, nutmeg and ginger to make gravy and simmer 3-4 minutes (without boiling). Serve gravy hot over the meat balls.

Venison Rice Meat Balls

1 lb. ground venison
1 cup parmesan cheese
1 tbsp. sugar
1 tsp. garlic powder
1 cup cooked rice
1/4 cup bacon fat
1 chopped onion
1/3 tsp. cinnamon
1/3 tsp. nutmeg salt and pepper
1 jar spaghetti sauce

Mix meat, rice, onion, sugar, parmesan and seasonings. Make into balls and saute until brown in bacon fat. Pour sauce over the mixture and bake 1 1/2 hrs. at 325 degrees. Add water as needed

Venison Rosemary Meat Loaf

2 lbs. ground venison
1/4 tbsp. Chili Powder
1/2 cup bacon fat
1 tbsp. salt
1 tsp. pepper
1 tsp. Garlic powder
1 lb. ground pork
1 jar Pasta sauce
1 cup milk
1/2 cup quick oats
1 egg
1 chopped med. Onion
2 tsp. Rosemary
1 tsp. MSG

Mix all ingredients except the Pasta sauce. Place in a loaf pan Bake at 350 degrees for 1 hour. Pour off fat, Cover with spaghetti sauce and serve

Venison Hamburgers

Venison is a Dry and Tough meat so for best results, you should add fat, preferably Bacon Fat to all Venison Hamburgers

Venison Hamburger

5 lbs. lean venison
2 tbsp. sage
1-1 1/2 cups bacon fat
1 tbsp. salt
1 tbsp. liquid smoke
5 tbsp. sugar
2 tbsp. pepper

Grind and thoroughly mix all ingredients, form into patties and saute. Wrap individually and it will keeps for 1 year in the freezer.

German Style Venison Hamburger

2 lbs. Ground Venison
1 Knockwurst, skinned and diced
Salt and pepper
4 ounces Bacon fat
1 small onion
1 tsp. Dill garlic powder to taste
3 ounces of Beer

Mix sausage and ground venison. Combine with remaining ingredients.
Brown until almost done. Add beer to deglaze the pan and make a sauce.

Polish Style Venison Hamburger

2 lbs. Ground Venison
1/2 Kielb.asa, skinned and diced
Salt and pepper
4 ounces Bacon fat
1 small onion
1 tsp. Dill garlic powder to taste
3 ounces of Beer

Mix sausage and ground venison. Combine with remaining ingredients.

Brown until almost done. Add beer to deglaze the pan and make a sauce.

French Style Venison Hamburger

2 lbs. Ground Venison
1/4 lb. Brie Cheese
Salt and pepper
4 ounces Bacon fat
1 small onion
1 tsp. Thyme garlic powder to taste
3 ounces of Red Wine

Grind and thoroughly mix all ingredients, form into patties and saute. Wrap individually and it will keeps for 1 year in the freezer.

Italian Style Venison Hamburger

2 lbs. Ground Venison
1/4 lb. Gorgonzola Cheese
Salt and pepper
4 ounces Bacon fat
1 small onion
1 tsp. Oregano garlic powder to taste
3 ounces of Red Wine

Mix sausage and ground venison. Combine with remaining ingredients.

Brown until almost done. Add wine to deglaze the pan and make a sauce.

Danish Style Venison Hamburger

2 lbs. Ground Venison
1/4 lb. Danish Blue Cheese
Salt and pepper
4 ounces Bacon fat
1 small onion
1 tsp. Thyme garlic powder to taste
3 ounces of Beer

Mix sausage and ground venison. Combine with remaining ingredients.

Brown until almost done. Add beer to deglaze the pan and make a sauce

Irish Style Venison Hamburger

2 lbs. Ground Venison
1/4 lb. Cheddar Cheese
Salt and pepper
4 ounces Bacon fat
1 small onion
1 tsp. Thyme garlic powder to taste
3 ounces of Stout

Grind and thoroughly mix all ingredients, form into patties and saute.

Wrap individually and it will keeps for 1 year in the freezer.

English Style Venison Hamburger

2 lbs. Ground Venison
1/4 lb. Cheddar Cheese
Salt and pepper
4 ounces Bacon fat
1 small onion
1 tsp. Thyme garlic powder to taste
3 ounces of Scotch Whiskey

Grind and thoroughly mix all ingredients, form into patties and saute.

Wrap individually and it will keeps for 1 year in the freezer.

Mexican Style Venison Hamburger

2 lbs. Ground Venison
1/4 lb. Jalapeno Pepper Cheese
1 tbsp.Salt
4 ounces Bacon fat
1 small onion
1 tbsp. Chili Powder garlic powder to taste
3 ounces of Corona Beer

Grind and thoroughly mix all ingredients, form into patties and saute.

Wrap individually and it will keeps for 1 year in the freezer.

American Style Venison Hamburger

2 lbs. Ground Venison
1/4 lb. Monterey Jack Cheese
Salt and pepper
4 ounces Bacon fat
1 small onion
1 tbsp. Chili Powder garlic powder to taste
3 ounces of Bourbon Whiskey

Grind and thoroughly mix all ingredients, form into patties and saute.

Wrap individually and it will keeps for 1 year in the freezer.

WOODCHUCK RECIPES

Woodchuck Hamburgers

Important Read This First:

Chef Gahagan says always marinate Woodchuck in Buttermilk and Meat Tenderizer for about three hours to clean taste. Then wash off the buttermilk and remarinate in wine and herbs if desired.

Ingredients

1 lb. Woodchuck Meat
1/2 cup Instant oatmeal
Salt and pepper
1 Egg
2 tbsp. Bacon fat
1/2 cup chopped onion

Directions

Clean, removing glands, and thoroughly wash woodchucks

Remove meat from bones and grind. Mix in quick oat meal (as a binder), onion, salt, pepper, egg, and bacon fat.

Form into patties; dip into egg; then dip in bread crumbs. Fry in hot fat until brown. Cover with currant jelly sauce and place in slow oven for 1 hour.

Woodchuck Stew

Important Read This First:

Chef Gahagan says always marinate Woodchuck in Buttermilk and Meat Tenderizer for about three hours to clean taste. Then wash off the buttermilk and remarinate in wine and herbs if desired.

Ingredients

1 1/2 lbs. Woodchuck
2 onions, sliced
1/2 cup chopped celery
Flour
Red wine and water
Salt and pepper
1/2 tsp. garlic powder
1 tsp. thyme
1 tsp. tarragon

Directions

Clean and thoroughly wash Woodchuck. Be sure to remove all glands.

Cut meat into serving pieces and soak overnight in a marinade of equal parts of water and red wine with one sliced onion and a little salt.

Drain, wash, and wipe. Parboil 20 minutes, drain, and cover with fresh boiling water. Add one sliced onion, thyme and tarragon, garlic, celery and salt and pepper to taste.

Cook until tender; then thicken gravy with flour or separate vegetables and blend them on high to create a natural gravy.

Sautéd Woodchuck

Important Read This First:

Chef Gahagan says always marinate Woodchuck in Buttermilk and Meat Tenderizer for about three hours to clean taste. Then wash off the buttermilk and remarinate in wine and herbs if desired.

Ingredients

3-4 1 woodchucks
Chicken stock
One chopped onion
1 tbsp. salt
1 cup flour
2 tbsp. fat
One half box mushrooms
One cup chopped celery

Directions

Clean woodchuck; remove glands.

Cut meat into 6 or 7 pieces. Parboil in chicken stock and celery for 1 hour.

Remove from broth and sauté in bacon fat with onions and mushrooms until brown.

Serves 6.

Woodchuck in Pasta Sauce

Important Read This First:

Chef Gahagan says always marinate Woodchuck in Buttermilk and Meat Tenderizer for about three hours to clean taste. Then wash off the buttermilk and remarinate in wine and herbs if desired.

Ingredients

2 woodchucks
Chicken stock
One chopped onion
1 tsp. salt
2 tbsp. Bacon fat
One box mushrooms
One cup chopped celery
2 cups spaghetti sauce

Directions

Clean woodchuck and be sure to remove glands.

Cut the meat into 6 or 7 pieces and simmer in chicken stock and celery for 1 hour.

Remove from broth and sauté in bacon fat with until brown. Cover with your favorite spaghetti sauce.

Sauté onions and mushrooms separately and serve as a side dish.

Serves 6.

WOODCOCK RECIPE

Woodcock Amandine

6 woodcock, or 12 dove or snipe split down back
1/4 cup flour
Salt and pepper
4 tbsp. Olive oil
1/2 cup Port wine
1/4 cup blanched, sliced almonds
1 tsp. Garlic Powder
1 tsp. MSG

Directions

Cover birds in flour, salt and pepper. Saute birds until nicely browned. Add wine, Garlic Powder, MSG, salt and pepper and water to cover.

Simmer for 20-30 minutes. Add almonds and cook for 5-10 minutes longer or until birds are fork tender. Allow 2 woodcock per serving.

Braised Woodcock

Ingredients:

4 Woodcock
1/2 tsp. Salt and Pepper or to taste
6 slices of crisp bacon
4 tbsp. Parmesan Cheese
4 slices of buttered Toast

Directions

Mix salt, pepper, Parmesan and Onion Powder and cover Woodcock inside and out. Cover each with a slice and a half of bacon and fasten with a toothpick. Broil at medium heat for 12 to 15 minutes on a side or until they are fork tender. Birds this small dry out quickly so baste often with bacon fat or olive oil.

Serve on buttered toast.

WILD TURKEY RECIPES

Wild Turkey differs fro Supermarket Tuurkey in three important ways. First, the Breast is much smaller or else it could not fly. Second, It has a slightly gamey taste and third, the meat, partiicularly the dark meat is tougher.

For these reasons, Chef Gahagan says always marinate Wild Turkey in Buttermilk and Meat Tenderizer for about three hours to clean taste and tenderize the meat. Then wash off the buttermilk and remarinate in wine and herbs if desired.

Wild Turkey in Bourbon and Apricot Cream

Ingredients

1 Wild Turkey Breast
2 cups chicken stock
1 onion cut up
6 chopped baby carrots
3 stalks of celery chopped
Salt and pepper to taste
1 tbsp. butter
1 tsp. MSG
6 ounces of heavy cream
3 ounces of bourbon
2 cans of Apricts drained

Directiona

Wash the Turkey breast. Simmer it briefly in chicken stock with carrots, celery, and onion until just tender. Then Saute it gently in butter. The time required will depend on the size of the breast and the desired amount of doneness.

While the Turkey is cooking blend a sauce of heavy cream, apricots, MSG and Bourbon. Heat to the desired thickness. Put the Turkey on a platter and pour the sauce over the pieces.

Turkey Brunswick Stew

This is an adaptation of the earliest true American Recipeand named after Brunswick County, Virginia

Ingredients

2-4 cups Turkey in bit size pieces
1 can Chicken stock or chicken broth
2 cup baby carrots
1 box frozen lima beans
1/2 cups chopped celery
1 chopped onion
2 tsp. Garlic Powder
1 tsp. Powdered Sage
1 1/2 tsp. MSG*
Water to cover
Salt and pepper to taste

Directions

Put all the ingredients in a pot and simmer until Turkey is well done.

Cool and put in refrigerator over night. Serve the next day. Mix in sherry at the end.

Butter Baked Turkey

Ingredients

2 lbs. scissored Turkey Breasts
Use 1 cup Butter or more
MSG
1 tbsp. Sugar
Salt and pepper to taste
1 cup Sherry

Directions

Put all ingredients in a pot or Casserole. Seal the top with aluminum foil, cover and cook until done.

Add MSG, salt, pepper and sugar to the butter in pot: mix to make a sauce and pour it over the Turkey.

Stir occasionally to prevent sticking

Turkey Breasts with Crumpled Bacon

Ingredients

4 Turkey legs or Breasts
Milk + 2 tbsp. according to
Directions

1 pkg. White sauce or Bechamel
3 tbsp. Bacon fat
1/2 lb. well done crumpled Bacon

Directions

Put Turkey in a Casserole dish with 2 tbsp. Bacon fat and bake for 1/2 hour.
Sauce, the Easy Way
Prepare packaged sauce according to directions. Use Bacon Fat instead of butter for added flavor. Stir in 3 extra ounces of milk and an extra tbsp. each of bacon fat and flour.
Add the crumpled bacon and the sauce is done.
Cover the Turkey with the sauce and serve when ready.

Easy Turkey Parmesan

Ingredients

2 pounds [1 kg] Turkey Breasts
4 tbsp. Butter
1 cup bread crumbs
1 cup grated Parmesan cheese
1 tsp. garlic powder
2 tbsp. Olive oil
1 tsp. Oregano
1 cup sliced onions

Directions

Cover Turkey breasts with melted butter.

Dredge buttered breasts in a mixture of bread Crumbs, oregano, garlic powder and parmesan cheese

Arrange Breasts in a Casserole. Add butter. Top with onion slices. Add remaining butter. Cover with foil and seal with Casserole dish top

Bake into a preheated 350°F [180°C] oven for 30 minutes or until Turkey is tender. Check to see if moisture is needed. If so, add wine or water.

Honey Mustard Wild Turkey

Ingredients

2 lbs. Turkey Breasts
1/2 cup Mustard (Dijon is best)
1/2 cup Honey
1/2 cup melted butter
1 tsp. MSG (MSG)
Bread Crumbs
2 tbsp. Olive oil

Directions

Mix MSG, mustard, honey and butter together

Coat or cover Breasts with all the Honey Mustard mix

Dip in Breadcrumbs

Put in an oven proof Casserole. Seal Casserole top with aluminum foil.

Bake until tender, about 30 minutes in a 325 oven. Correct seasonings.

Add milk if necessary.

Easy Wild Turkey Cacciatore

Ingredients

2 lbs. Wild Turkey
Salt and pepper to taste
Chicken stock or a can of chicken broth
1 tbsp. Flour
1 1/2 cups baby carrots
1 box frozen Spinach
1/2 cups chopped celery
1 chopped onion
2 tsp. Garlic Powder
1/2 tsp. Powdered Oregano
1 tsp. MSG*
Water to cover
1/2 cup sherry*
Salt and pepper to taste

Directions

Put all the ingredients in a pot and simmer until turkey is well done. Cool and put in refrigerator over night.

Heat and serve the next day. Mix in sherry at the end.

Wild Turkey Curry

Ingredients:

2 cups of cooked turkey cut into bite size pieces
2 packages of Curry sauce*
2 sticks of butter
1 tsp. garlic powder
1 tsp. onion powder
1 tsp. sugar
2 tsp. paprika
2-3 tbsp. Curry powder (if needed)
1-1/2 cup Raisins and/or scissored prunes

Directions

Make a Curry sauce according to package directions or follow the recipe below. If your store does not have a curry sauce mix, buy a white sauce mix and add Curry powder

Mix raisins and scissored prunesinti sauce.

Put turkey in a serving dish, add sauce and decorate with paprika and/or pieces of canned apricots, mushrooms or peaches as you desire. Heat until it starts to simmer and serve.

*Recipe for Curry sauce from scratch.

Melt 5 tbsp. butter in a double boiler. Add 6 tbsp. Flour. Heat and stir together into a roux.

Slowly add 2 cups of milk stirring continually. Add salt and pepper to taste and 1/2 tsp. Garlic and Onion powder, raisins and prunes and 2-3 tbsp. Curry Powder.

Easy Turkey Marmelade (a l'Orange)

2 cups of Turkey Breast Leftovers, scissored into bite size pieces
2 cup melted Butter
1 can chicken broth Paprika for color
1 jar Marmalade
1 cup Heavy cream
1 tsp. MSG

Directions

Firstprepare the Marmalade Sauce. Puree marmalade, frozen orange juice, cream and MSG on high. Then, slowly simmer until sauce thickened. Do NOT boil.

The Turkey: Sprinkle turkey pieces with paprika and place them in a pot with chicken broth. Cook until tender. Drain and freeze stock for future use. Add butter and stir to eliminate sticking. Put the Turkey in a Casserole

Pot dish, top with Marmalade Cream Sauce and serve.

Easy Roman Style Turkey

Ingredients

4 slices Turkey breast
4 slices Procuito or deli ham slices Mozzarella
4 tsp. Parmesan Cheese
2 tbsp. Olive oil

Directions

Mix spices, oregano, garlic, salt pepper Brown Chicken pieces very gently.

When half done, top chicken with deli ham, Mozzarella and parmesan cheese.

Cover pan and continue to saute gently until done.

Serve with rice.

Easy Turkey in Sour Cream Sauce

Ingredients

2 cupa Turkey in bite size pieces
4 ounces of butter
Flour
Salt and pepper
1 pint sour cream
1 onion
1 box sliced mushrooms
1 chopped green or red bell pepper

Directions

Marinate Turkey in buttermilk and tenderizer and cut into 4 Portion size pieces. Wash off Buttermilk

Next dip in flour and brown gently in butter in a frying pan. Deglaze pan with a small amount of water.

Place this with Chicken in a large buttered pot and sprinkle with salt and pepper. Put enough sour cream in pot to make its depth 1 inch and add butter.

Cover and bake at 350 degrees F. for 3/4 hrs. or until pieces are tender.

Add milk to sour cream as needed to maintain consistency.

Saute the onion, the chopped pepper and in olive oil. Add to sour cream and cover birds before serving.

Turkey Stroganoff

Ingredients

2 lbs. Wild Turkey in bite size pieces
4 ounces of butter
Flour
Salt and pepper
1 pint sour cream
1 onion
1 box sliced mushrooms
1 tsp. Garlic Powder
1 tsp. MSG.

Directions

Clean and wash Turkey pieces.

Next dip Turkey pieces in flour and brown gently in butter in a good size pot.

Place the Turkey in a large pot and sprinkle with seasonings.

Add the onion and the mushrooms and Saute until Chicken is tender

Add sour cream to the pot and cover and bake at 300 degrees F. for 1/4 hr. to meld the flavors. Add milk to sour cream as needed to maintain consistency.

Turkey Mexicana

Ingredients:

Young Turkey Breasts divided into 4 portions tbsp. butter
4 tbsp. Salsa (your choice of "hot")
1 tsp. Dark Rum

Directions:

Scissored Turkey breasts into bite size pieces.

Cook Turkey and butter in a pot, Stirring occasionally so it does not stick together. Add salsa and rum when chicken is Done.

Easy Turkey Zucchini

Ingredients:

4 Turkey breasts, cut to one portion size
4 tbsp. Bacon Fat
2 cans Zucchini in tomato sauce
2 tbsp. Parmesan Cheese
1 tsp. garlic
2 tbsp. Port wine

Directions

Put Bacon Fat and turkey Breasts in a pot with butter and cook until tender. Turn Tutkey over at least once. Mix Zucchini with seasonings and wine. Top the Turkey pieces with zucchini mix, heat until warm and then top with parmesan.

Easy Pineapple Turkey

Ingredients

4 quarter pound pieces of leftover Turkey breast
2 tbsp. melted Butter
Salt and pepper to taste
1 can Pineapple Chunks
2 tsp. Cinnamon
1 tsp. MSG

Directions

Drain pineapple juice and mix with cinnamon and MSG.

Sprinkle turkey pieces with salt and pepper, place them in a skillet with salt, pepper, MSG and melted butter and saute until tender, turning frequently.

Place Chicken pieces in a Casserole dish, top with Pineapple Chunks and cover with cinnamon/pineapple Sauce.

Bake at 350 F for 15 minutes and serve.

Tijuana Turkey

Ingredients:

4 quarter pound pieces of Turkey Breast
4 tbsp. Bacon Fat
1 cup Chicken/Turkey Stock
6 tbsp. Tomato Sauce
6 oz. Heavy Cream
1 tbsp. Chili Powder
1 tsp. Adobe powder

Directions:

Scissor Turkey breasts into bite size pieces.
Cook Turkey and bacon fat in a pot,

Stirring occasionally so it does not stick to the bottomgether.

Add chicken stock and cook for 15 minutes more

Stir in cream, Tomato Sauce, Chili powder and Adobe Seasonings when chicken is done.

Turkeuy in Plum Sause

Ingredients

2 cups of turkey Breasts cut into bite size pieces
1/2 cup melted Butter
1 can Plums
12 Prunes
1 cup Heavy cream
1 tsp. MSG
Salt and pepper to taste

Directions

First prepare the Plum Sauce.

Drain Plums, remove any pits and puree with Cream, Prunes and MSG on high. Then, slowly simmer until thickened.

The Turkey

Sprinkle turkey pieces with paprika, place them in a skillet with melted butter and mix.

Saute pieces of Turkey until tender.

Place them in a Casserole dish and top with Plum Cream Sauce. Heat and serve.

Wild Turkey with Wild Rice

A lot of Recipe Writers think that having long complicated Recipes makes them look more knowledgeable. Forget it. Always search for the "Easy" version of a recipe on any Search Engine

Ingredients

1 Roast Chicken cut up
1/2 cup flour
1 cup raw wild rice
1 can cream of chicken soup
1 can cream of mushroom soup
1 can mushrooms
2 cups water
1 cup Port wine
Water chestnuts
1 pkg. instant onion soup mix

Directions

Flour Turkeuy Pieces.

Mix rice, canned soups, water, wine, mushrooms and water chestnuts in a Casserole. Add Turkey pieces. Sprinkle with onion soup mix. Cover and bake 2 hours at 300 degrees.

Wild Turkey Breast Pecan

Ingredients

2 4 oz pieses o Turkey Breast
4 tbsp. butter
3 1/2 ounces [100 g] Pecan bits
1/2 cup honey
Salt and pepper to taste
2 cups chicken/turkey stock

Directions

Saute Pecans in 1 tbsp. butter

Remove Pecans, add the rest of the butter and sauté Turkey Breasts until done.

If you have a tough old bird, parboil the turkey in stock wit tenderizer

Add the honey and the Pecans back into the pan and stir together.

Put turkey pieces on a serving plate. Then deglaze the pan and pour the Pecan, Honey/Butter sauce over the Breasts.

Turkey VB

Ingredients

4 skinless, boneless chicken breasts
1 can of Cream of Chicken Soup
1/2 cup V8
1/2 up each of Peas and Corn
2 tsp. Dill.
4 small Artichoke hearts (from a can)
1/2 tsp. Pepper

Directions

Saute chicken breasts until they are well browned on both sides.

Add the soup, V8, corn, pepper and dill to the pan and bring to a simmer.

Cover and cook for 5 minutes or until the chicken is cooked through.

Top with the small Artichoke Hearts and serve.

Easy Turkey V8

Ingredients

4 Skinless 4 oz pieces of Turkey Breast
1 cup V8
1 can Italian Style tomatoes
1 can corn
2 tsp. Dill.
4 small Artichoke hearts (from a can)
1/2 tsp. Pepper

Directions

Saute c\turkey breasts until they are browned on both sides.

Blend the V8, tomatoes, pepper and dill on high, Then add corn. Add turkey to pot with the mix and bring to a simmer. Cover and cook until the turkey icken is tender.

Top with the small Artichoke Hearts and serve.

Turkey au Vin

This is based on one of the most famous Recipes in the worls—Coq au Vin

Ingredients

2-3 lbs. Turkey
1 tomato
4 cups Port wine
1 tbsp. Sage
2 tsp. Thyme
1 tsp. MSG salt and pepper to taste
2 tsp. MSP

Directions

Put all the ingredients in a pot and simmer until the turkey falls off the bones.100 Serve with bacoq aoby carrots

Coq au Vin a l'orange

Ingredients

2 lbs. Turkey meat
1 tomato
3 cups Port wine
1 cup frozen orange juice
1 tsp. MSG salt and pepper to taste

Directions

Put all the ingredients in a pot and simmer until the turkey falls off the bone.

Turkey in Pineapple Cream

Ingredients

2 cups of Turkey Breasts cut into bite size pieces
2 tbsp. melted Butter
Salt and pepper to taste
1 can Pineapple Chunks
1 cup chicken/turkey stock
1 cup Heavy Cream
1 tsp. MSG

Directions

First prepare the Pineapple Sauce.

Drain Pineapple Juice with cream.

The Turkey

Oil a large pan. Sprinkle chicken pieces with salt and pepper and saute until tender, turning frequently. If bird is tough, add chicken stock and simmer.

When turkey is tender, add the Pineapple/cream Sauce and mix thoroughly. Heat until it starts to simmer and serve.

Wild Turkey Mona Loa

Mona Loa is a volcano, hencethe firey taste

Ingredients

2 cups of Turkey Breasts cut into bite size pieces
2 tbsp. melted Butter
Salt and pepper to taste
1 can Pineapple Chunks
1/2 cup Salsa (your choice of "hot"
1 can corn drained
1 tsp. MSG

Directions

First prepare the Pineapple Sauce.

Drain Pineapple Juice and mix chunks with Salsa and MSG.

The Turkey

Oil a large pan. Sprinkle turkey pieces with salt and pepper and saute until tender, turning frequently.

Add the Pineapple/Salsa Sauce and mix thoroughly. Heat until it starts tp simmer and serve.

Wild Turkey Acapulco

Ingredients

1 11/2 lbs. Wild turkey Breast
1 jar salsa (your choice of hot)
1 can Cheddar Cheese Soup
1 can Small Artichoke Hearts
4 tbsp. butter
1 can water

Directions

Preheat oven to 300F
Put butter and chicken in pot and saute until golden
Mix Soup, Artichoke hearts and Salsa and add to the pot.
Bake at 300 F for 1 hour.

Wild Turkey in Artichoke Honey Sauce

Ingredients

2 cups of Wild Turkey Breasts cut into bite size pieces
1 1/2 cups heavy cream
1 can small or medium artichoke hearts
Paprika for color
2 tsp. Garlic Powder
2 tsp. MSG
4 ounces of honey extra milk

Directions

Blend Artichokes, cream, honey and Garlic Powder on high.
Place Turkey pieces in a Casserole and cover with sauce.
Then, slowly simmer until Turkey is tender. Add milk as needed to maintain moisture

Wild Turkey in Apricot Sauce

Ingredients

2 cups of Chicken Breasts in bite size pieces
1/4 cup melted Butter
1 1/4 olive oil
Paprika for color
1 can Apricots or fresh Apricots if available
2 cups Light Cream
1/4 cup Honey
1 tsp. MSG

Directions

First prepare the Apricot Sauce.

Drain Apricots and blend with honey and cream and MSG on high. Then, pour into a pot and slowly simmer until thickened.

The Turkey

Sprinkle Turkey pieces with paprika, place them in a skillet with melted butter and oil mix.

Sauté pieces of Turkey in oil until tender. Cover with top if necessary. Add butter at end.

Place them in a Casserole dish and top with Apricot Cream Sauce. Heat until warm and serve.

Wild Turkey with Apples

Editor's Note: In France, this is called Poulet Normand.

Ingredients

2 Turkey Thighs or I breast
4 Apples
1 cup light cream
1 cup milk
1 tsp. MSG
2 tsp. Oregano leaves
2 tsp. Sugar
2 tbsp. Brandy or Rum
Salt and pepper to taste.

Directions

Slice apples and remove pits

Mix Oregano, applesauce, milk, Garlic powder and cream

Put Thighs in a casserole dish and cover with the sauce mix.

Put a layer of Aluminum foil over Casserole dish and cover. Cook at 350 F until Turkey is tender. Add milk if necessary. Add Brandy to the sauce 5 minutes before done

Baked Turkey Bacon

Ingredients:

1 lb. Thin Sliced Turkey Breasts
1 pkg. White Sauce
8 slices Bacon
1 tsp. MSG
2 tsp. Sage
Salt and pepper to taste

Directions:

Microwave Bacon until crisp
Preheat oven to 350 F.
Prepare White Sauce according to pkg. Directions use Bacon Fat instead of butter and mix in MSG and Sage.
Oil a casserole dish with bacon fat. Put in turkey slices. Top with white sauce and crumpled bacon. Bake until done

Ingredients

4 Sliced Turkey Breasts
1 can sliced Peaches
1 cup light cream
1 tsp. MSG
2 tsp. Oregano
1 tsp. Garlic or Sage powder

Ingredients

Saute pieces of Turkey until tender.
Mix Oregano OR Sage powder with Garlic powder and cream
Next. alternate layers of Turkey and peach slices in a Casserole dish. Cover with cream sauce.
Heat until sauce begins to simmer and serve.

Roast Wild Turkey

Ingredients

1 Wild Turkey, cleaned and washed
1 tbsp. salt
1/2 tsp. pepper
5 stalks celery
6 bacon slices
6 bacon slices done to a crisp
1 chopped large onion
6 baby carrots
1 can mushrooms
1 cup Sherry
One cup heavy cream
Wild rice

Directions

Brush Turkey with Bacon Fat.

Sprinkle salt and pepper on Turkey.

Put onion, mushrooms, carrots and celery in bird's cavity. Place breast side down on a rack in the roasting pan. Dribble remaining bacon fat over breast and place bacon strips on top of bird.

Turn bird breast side up 20 minutes before it is done and cover breast with bacon slices. Bake at 350 degrees for 20 minutes per pound or until bird is 140 F with a meat thermometer in the breast. DO NOT OVERCOOK.

Deglaze pan, pour off the fat. Remove vegetables and blend on high with deglazed pan juices. Add sherry and heavy cream. Add grapes to sauce if desired, Serve with wild rice.

Wild Turkey Breasts for 6

Important Read This First:

Chef Gahagan says always marinate Wild Turkey pieces in Buttermilk and Meat Tenderizer for about three hours. Then wash off the buttermilk and remarinate in wine and herbs if desired.

Ingredients

Wild Turkey Breasts for 6
Salt and pepper to taste
Flour
Cooking Oil
1 can mandarin oranges
2 cans of mushroom soup
1 cup heavy cream
2 ounces Brandy
1 tsp. sugar

Preheat oven to 350 degrees F.

Coat Breasts in oil. Sprinkle seasoned salt and pepper on breasts and flour them.

Brown lightly in a skillet with cooking oil; then put in a greased baking dish and set aside.

Combine the 2 cans of soup with the heavy cream in a saucepan and heat.

Drain the cans of Mandarin orange. Add the mandarin oranges to the soup mix and pour over Wild Turkey and bake 1/2 hour at 300 F. Mix in brandy before serving.

Wild Turkey in Sour Cream

Important Read This First:

Chef Gahagan says always marinate Wild Turkey pieces in Buttermilk and Meat Tenderizer for about three hours. Then wash off the buttermilk and remarinate in wine and herbs if desired.

Ingredients

Wild Turkey Pieces for six
Flour
Salt and pepper
1 pint sour cream
1 onion
1/2 box sliced mushrooms
1 chopped bell pepper

Directions

Wild Turkey can be very dry.

Scissor enough meat for six into 1" square pieces and marinate in buttermilk with added meat tenderizer. Wash off buttermilk and wipe thoroughly.

Next dip in flour and sauté gently in butter in a pot with onions, mushrooms and pepper. Deglaze pan with a small amount of water and add the turkey pieces, salt pepper and sour cream.

Cover and bake at 350 degrees F. until pieces are tender. Add milk to sour cream as needed to maintain consistency.

Italian Wild Turkey

Important Read This First:

Chef Gahagan says always marinate Wild Turkey pieces in Buttermilk and Meat Tenderizer for about three hours. Then wash off the buttermilk and remarinate in wine and herbs if desired.

Ingredients

1 Wild turkey meat for six
1 medium onion
2 green peppers i/2 tsp. garlic powder
1 tbsp. sesame oil
1 tsp. salt
1/4 cup olive oil i jar spaghetti sauce
One half cup parmesan cheese
1 tbsp. sugar
1 tsp. oregano salt and pepper to taste

Brown turkey pieces very gently. Deglaze pan; mix vegetables, seasonings and spaghetti sauce, and parmesan cheese sauce in a pot: add Turkey with deglazed juices. Simmer till done adding water if necessary.

Serve with rice.

Braised Wild Turkey

Chef Gahagan says always marinate Wild Turkey pieces in Buttermilk and Meat Tenderizer for about three hours. Then wash off the buttermilk and remarinate in wine and herbs if desired.

Ingredients

Enough Turkey pieces for four
3 tbsp. bacon fat
1 can chicken broth
1 med. onion, cut into pieces
2 stalks celery, chopped
6 small carrots
2 ounces of ham
1 tsp. sugar
4 ounces of sherry

Directions

Make a broth using canned chicken broth onion, celery, carrots and ham.

Brush Wild Turkey with bacon fat and brown in a pot roast pot.

Add broth and contents and cook until tender.

Remove bird pieces and blend vegetables with liquid in a blender to make a sauce.

Add sherry to sauce, place bird on platter and pour sauce over meat.

Italian Wild Turkey

Important Read This First:

Chef Gahagan says always marinate Wild Turkey pieces in Buttermilk and Meat Tenderizer for about three hours. Then wash off the buttermilk and remarinate in wine and herbs if desired.

Ingredients

1 lb. Wild turkey meat (for four)
1 medium onion
1 green pepper
1 tsp. garlic powder
1/4 cup olive oil
1 jar pasta sauce
1/2 cup parmesan cheese
1 tbsp. sugar
1 1/2 tsp. oregano salt and pepper to taste

Directions

Saute turkey pieces very gently in a pot. Add vegetables, seasonings and spaghetti sauce, and parmesan cheese sauce to the pot. Simmer till done adding water if necessary.
Serve with rice.

Easy Apricot Turkey

Important Read This First:

Chef Gahagan says always marinate Wild Turkey pieces in Buttermilk and Meat Tenderizer for about three hours. Then wash off the buttermilk and remarinate in wine and herbs if desired.

Ingredients

One Wild Turkey cleaned and washed
2 cup chicken broth
3 onions cut up
1 cup Stuffing mix
6 baby carrots
3 stalks of celery chopped
8 bacon Slices
1 apple chopped
Salt and pepper

Directions

Mix vegetables, broth and fruit and stuff turkey.

Lay bacon slices on top of breast. Cook the birds slowly at 300-350 degrees F. Wild Turkey is much drier than supermarket turkey. Be sure to baste often with a mixture of melted butter and broth. The time required will depend on the size of the bird and the desired amount of doneness.

Turkey will need 20 minute t the pound. at 350 degrees F.

While the Turkey is cooking make a sauce of one jar of apricot preserves, dried apricots, 1 cup cream and 1 tbsp. brandy

Serve the sauce with the turkey

Turkey and Wild Rice

Important Read This First:

Chef Gahagan says always marinate Wild Turkey pieces in Buttermilk and Meat Tenderizer for about three hours. Then wash off the buttermilk and remarinate in wine and herbs if desired.

Ingredients

Turkey pieces for 6, cut up and floured
1 cup raw wild rice
1 can cream of chicken soup
1 can cream of mushroom soup
1 can mushrooms
2 1/2 cups water
1 pkg. instant onion soup mix

Directions

Lightly sauté Turkey pieces

Mix rice, canned soups, water, mushrooms and water chestnuts in 9x13 glass casserole. Add sautéed turkey. Sprinkle with onion soup mix. Cover lightly with foil. Bake 2-2 1/2 hours at 300 degrees.

Wild Turkey in Irish Cream

Important Read This First:

Chef Gahagan says always marinate Wild Turkey pieces in Buttermilk and Meat Tenderizer for about three hours. Then wash off the buttermilk and remarinate in wine and herbs if desired.

Ingredients

Enough Turkey White Meat for 6
1 tsp. salt
1/4 tsp. pepper
1/4 cup melted butter
3 bacon slices done to a crisp
1 med. onion
1 (3 oz.) can mushrooms
1 cup water
1/2 cup Irish Cream Whiskey
One half cup heavy cream
Seedless Grapes
Rice

Directions

Brush turkey with melted butter and sprinkle with salt and pepper. Put in a pot and sauté gently. Add the rest of the vegetables, water and butter.

Simmer until tender.

Remove turkey pieces to a serving platter. Blend residue of vegetables on high with cream and Irish Cream for a sauce. Add grapes,
Serve with rice.

www.ingramcontent.com/pod-product-compliance
Ingram Content Group UK Ltd.
Pitfield, Milton Keynes, MK11 3LW, UK
UKHW041949190726
13854UKWH00004B/1877

9 781453 567326